Butterflies
and Sweaty Palms

25 SURE-FIRE WAYS
to SPEAK and PRESENT
with CONFIDENCE

Judy Apps

Crown House Publishing Limited
www.crownhouse.co.uk
www.crownhousepublishing.com

First published by

Crown House Publishing Ltd
Crown Buildings, Bancyfelin, Carmarthen, Wales, SA33 5ND, UK
www.crownhouse.co.uk

and

Crown House Publishing Company LLC
6 Trowbridge Drive, Suite 5, Bethel, CT 06801-2858, USA
www.crownhousepublishing.com

British Library Cataloguing-in-Publication Data
A catalogue entry for this book is available from the British Library.

ISBN
ISBN 978-184590736-5 (print)
ISBN 978-184590771-6 (mobi)
ISBN 978-184590772-3 (ePub)

LCCN 2011938912

Printed and bound in the UK by
Bell & Bain Ltd, Glasgow

To all who have felt fearful before speaking

Contents

Introduction

'You've either got it or you haven't,' that's what people say.

'Either you're a good public speaker or you're not.'

'Speakers are born and not made.'

That's bad news if you don't feel you are a born speaker. Speaking is an essential skill. It isn't only those occasions on the podium or even the oft-dreaded wedding speech; the ability to communicate under pressure is required in countless different situations – for informal presentations, meetings, interviews, key leadership moments, tackling a difficult situation with a colleague or even asking someone out on a date.

If you don't feel confident about your ability such moments can be a real challenge and create a lot of sweat, anxiety and sleepless nights. But they are hard to avoid completely.

So, should you give up now?

No, not at all.

Just read a little bit further ...

> O God of second chances and new beginnings, here I am.
> Again.
>
> Nancy Spiegelberg

PART I

Exploring the Territory

CHAPTER 1

Is It Really Possible – For Me?

> Here is Edward Bear, coming downstairs now, bump, bump, bump, on the back of his head, behind Christopher Robin. It is, as far as he knows, the only way of coming downstairs, but sometimes he feels that there really is another way, if only he could stop bumping for a minute and think of it.
>
> A. A. Milne, *Winnie-the-Pooh*

Lots of books have been written on public speaking and presenting; perhaps you've read some of them. Maybe up till now none of those books has made much difference. You might ask yourself if it's really possible to speak well in public – for you.

So straight away I want to tell you the answer is yes.

Yes, it's possible.

It's possible for you.

You really can learn how to perform well in public. You can learn what to do to overcome performance anxiety even if you think you have tried everything and have completely run out of ideas.

What gives me the confidence that it's possible for you? Well, because I have witnessed many people succeed. Over the years I have coached hundreds of people on public speaking and confidence, and many started with little hope. My Voice of Influence workshops have been attended by some who could scarcely get themselves inside the door but edged in holding on to the walls with fear. And those very same people by the end of the next day stood up and gave a speech – without notes – that connected powerfully with the audience.

I have worked with people one-to-one who have told me at the outset that their issue goes beyond fear: 'This is not just fear, it's a phobia,' they say. Those same people learn in a few sessions how to perform with assurance. One person had actually fainted from anxiety the last time she'd had to give a presentation for her corporation. Very soon after we had worked together she went on to give a successful presentation to an audience of two hundred potential investors.

I am sure that you too would like to be able to perform with assurance and confidence. But the truth may be that you are worried and frightened. You tell yourself not to be but nothing ever changes. Maybe too you have heard promises from teachers and trainers that didn't lead to any positive results for you.

So what will be different this time?

Firstly, it's not just about learning what to do. You probably have a good idea *what* to do already. Even if you feel less than confident about your material, the finer points of running a PowerPoint presentation or the protocols of a formal speech, even if you worry about forgetting things or looking stupid or making mistakes, I'm convinced you have watched enough people speak either live or on screen to know broadly what to do. You are probably also sufficiently aware of the pitfalls to know what *not* to do.

The problem is that even with this knowledge you can't do it. You've already tried to do what you see good speakers do and it hasn't worked for you. The reason it hasn't worked I suspect is that you don't believe it's possible for you. It's your self-belief that lets you down.

What you'll learn

> If you think you are too small to be effective, you have never been in bed with a mosquito.
>
> Betty Reese

This time you'll get to the root of it. This book will help you in easy steps to gain the self-belief to speak brilliantly.

You'll learn:

- The one thing you need to know to stop feeling alone and hopeless.

- The four 'common-sense' strategies you're probably using right now and why they never work.

- Why most of the advice you're getting from well-meaning professionals and self-help books is actually making it harder to perform well.

- Why 'working' at improving your performance is never successful and what to do about it.

- How to overcome your self-defeating belief that it's just not possible, and create the mindset that will allow you to get exactly what you want.

- How to make sure you're in the right frame of mind – every time.

- How to come alive when you're speaking instead of dying on your feet.

- What to say and what not to say to make sure that the audience loves you and listens to every word you say.

- How to ensure that you hit the ground running whenever you speak.

The book is in two parts: Part I introduces you to some of the tools and Part II contains 25 sure-fire strategies for overcoming performance anxiety. When you get to Part II you might want to read straight through from beginning to end on a first reading, or you may prefer to browse to see which strategies jump out at you and practise those first. You can then go through Part II again and learn the strategies one by one. Some will be immediately useful and others might take a bit of practice. Sometimes those are the very ones that will become your favourites.

Each strategy in Part II is introduced and then the process is laid out step by step. At the end of each strategy there are notes or case studies based on the experiences of others who have done the exercises. These notes will guide you to explore various options to make the strategies work for you – even those that seem less easy at first. This makes it more like my working with you in real life: we are all different and sometimes exercises work better if they are 'tweaked' a little to suit you.

Keep the book by you and consult it every time you have a question you can't answer or whenever you need a bit of extra help. You can also contact me at info@voiceofinfluence.co.uk if you can't find the answer.

The journey starts here. If you are impatient you can go straight to Part II and get started on the strategies! Come back to Part I though – it's an important part of the process.

Your success will depend less on hard work than on your willingness to try something different. Listen to this cautionary tale:

The Fly

In our kitchen we mostly keep the window shut and the door wide open in summer. I often find dead flies on our south-facing windowsill. Each fly tries to escape to the garden through the pane of glass. Again and again it flies towards the light against the glass; it buzzes furiously and again and again I hear the small bang of its body hitting the pane. I sense the life and death exertion: 'Again! Again! Try harder, try harder!' But it is never going to succeed and the effort allows no hope of survival. The fly is doomed.

If it could just back away from the seductive light of the window and change its strategy for only a moment it would find the huge gaping door to take it into the world outside. With simple ease in just a few seconds it would be free. But it never can. It has condemned itself to endless effort towards a doomed goal.

Are you like the fly banging at a closed window with your efforts to overcome performance anxiety? If you try what you have always tried you are probably going to get the result you've had so far.

Relax. Breathe again. Sometimes it's about going about something differently. Have a look around you. The door to freedom is open. All you need to do is step through …

CHAPTER 2

Let's Look At This Thing Called Fear

A young actor confessed to an older actor before a performance that he had nervous butterflies in his stomach. 'I don't expect you get those any more, do you?' he asked.

The older actor looked at him with the hint of a smile and replied, 'Oh yes, I still get them; but I don't try and kill them. I've taught them to fly in formation.'

Fear is not bad of itself. It keeps us out of danger so that we don't get too close to a cliff edge or lean into a fire. But our fear is sometimes out of date and based on a strange assortment of emotional data from the past. Human beings do not have to be in real danger to set off feelings of fear.

So let's start at the beginning by looking at fear itself, not because we want to focus on the negative but in the spirit of kissing the frog that's going to turn into a prince.

It feels lonely ... but is it?

When you are afraid, it can be a lonely feeling. You feel inadequate and abnormal. You convince yourself that you are the *only* person in existence who feels this way. It seems that the *whole world* can do this thing and you're the only person who can't.

Well, I'm sorry to disappoint you if you get a kick out of feeling unusual.

This isn't unusual: it's common.

> The biggest big business in America is not steel, automobiles, or television. It is the manufacture, refinement and distribution of anxiety.
>
> Eric Sevareid, American news commentator

People get fearful all the time and they are afraid of a lot of things! A BBC survey in 2006 of people's twenty worst fears[1] came up with an extraordinary mix of scare-making things from buttons, balloons and ice-lolly sticks to coleslaw, feathers and the letter Y! Fear of public speaking is certainly not unusual. One survey in 1993 asked people 'about the things of which nightmares are made' and they mentioned fear of heights, deep water, insects, financial problems, sickness, death and much else besides.[2] But the most common fear of all was speaking before a group. It came out right at the top of the list way above fear of death!

It is true you may have a gentler word for it, there may be a number of other factors involved and of course technique is important too, but the basis of most performance discomfort is fear. In fact, it's the biggest single factor preventing us from achieving just about anything.

'More good creative ability is wasted due to fear than anything else I can think of,' says the author of *Creative Thinking*, Michael LeBoeuf: 'People with good voices are afraid to sing. People with artistic talent hide their

---

[1] See http://news.bbc.co.uk/1/hi/magazine/4849832.stm, 30 March 2006 (accessed 11 July 2011).

[2] Bruskin-Goldring Research (1993). America's number 1 fear: Public speaking. Edison, NJ: Bruskin-Goldring.

paintings rather than risk ridicule. People who love to write are too embarrassed to show their writing to anyone.'[3]

What are your main fears about public speaking?

- Fear of being looked at?

- Fear of not knowing enough?

- Fear of not being able to express in words what you want to say?

- Fear of drying up?

- Fear of your voice sounding all wrong?

- Fear of going red and blushing?

- Fear of being judged and found wanting?

- Fear of being vulnerable to what people might say or do?

- Fear of revealing things about yourself that you don't want people to know?

- Fear of forgetting something important or losing track?

- Fear of getting flustered with unexpected questions or interruptions?

- Fear triggered by remembering bad occasions in the past?

- Fear that you won't measure up to other people?

- Fear of looking foolish?

- Fear of not being good enough?

- Fear of the feeling of panic?

- Fear of getting frightened?

- ....

- ....

Are your fears included here? I've left a space for you to add your own. What frightens you the most?

---

[3] Michael LeBoeuf (1994). *Creative Thinking: How to Generate Ideas and Turn Them into Successful Reality*. London: Piatkus Books.

Fear and the famous

> It plagues me. I'm standing in the wings with the sweat pour-
> ing off me thinking what on earth am I doing?
>
> Sinéad Cusack, speaking about stage fright

It's not just ordinary people who get nervous: it's everyone! You only have to use your eyes and ears to know that it's true. Switch on the television news and watch presidents and prime ministers as they come into the public gaze. Before they descend the stairs of the recently arrived aeroplane the men adjust their ties and touch their pockets and the women smooth their skirts and play with their hair. Do you think they didn't check their appearance before the aircraft door opened? Of course they did. This fidgeting is just nerves.

Watch well-known speakers: how they compulsively straighten their conference papers or touch their faces. Watch actors being interviewed: how they over-laugh and over-enthuse. Watch politicians in important debates: how their gestures become stiff and their voices narrowed. Then watch them put on the spot: how they blink and fidget and tap or clutch their hands. Think they aren't nervous?

So take note of this important observation:

**The extent of your nerves bears little relation
to the amount of talent you have.**

Many famous people have been famously frightened:

- The actor John Cleese confided that before *The Frost Report*, which was transmitted live, he could not have been more afraid if he had been in a bullring with an angry bull.

- The generous-sized and usually cheery actor Patricia Routlege was discovered before one of her solo spots in *Victoria Wood as Seen on TV* shaking in terror underneath the costume racks in the dressing room.

- TV personality Stephen Fry gave up fronting the BAFTA awards confessing that he suffered extreme stage fright prior to his appearances.

- The great actor Sir Laurence Olivier was so struck with nerves in one run at London's National Theatre that he had to have the stage manager push him onstage every night.

- The legendary cellist Pablo Casals suffered so much from clammy hands at his Viennese debut that the cello bow shot out of his grasp during an early flourish and hit someone in the ninth row of the audience.

- The singer Barbra Streisand, after forgetting one of her lyrics during a Central Park concert, stopped performing live for almost *three decades*.

- The film star Lauren Bacall initially adopted her seductive trademark look – where she presses her chin against her chest to face the camera and tilts her eyes upward – as a tactic to stop her nervous quivering.

- The singer Bruce Springsteen claims to get excited rather than frightened but admits to being physically sick before performances.

Shall I go on? It's not just actors and musicians – we meet performance fear everywhere:

- The broadcaster Sheridan Morley, who wrote the news in the early days of television, was once called upon at short notice to read the bulletin. His fear got the better of him and afterwards he says that many people wrote in to give him advice on his Parkinson's disease!

- The boxer George Foreman recounting his famous fight with Joe Frazier remembers that his knees were knocking so much he just hoped that Joe wouldn't glance down and realise his advantage. 'Fear is everything,' he said. 'It's not the fight you lose, it's yourself.'

- Go back in history and you discover the British Prime Minister William Gladstone taking laudanum – or opium tincture – before important political speeches to steady his nerves.

- In the popular television programme we watch hopeful entrepreneurs arrive in the 'Dragons' Den' and quake visibly or even dry up completely before the multimillionaire potential investors.

The American philosopher Ralph Waldo Emerson writing back in the nineteenth century declared that 'Fear stops more people than anything else in the world.' Fear is widespread. Fear assails us all.

> Most people think that courage is the absence of fear. The absence of fear is not courage; the absence of fear is some kind of brain damage.
> M. Scott Peck, *Further Along the Road Less Traveled*

But note this first glimmer of light: even though famous and talented people clearly feel fear *they are nevertheless successful*. So it is clearly *possible* to feel frightened and yet to perform with distinction. You certainly cannot claim that fear equals failure – all the people mentioned above have won through. They understood the most important lesson of performing: it's not a case of *either* feel fear *or* perform well; it's *both* feel fear *and* perform well. Both/and – that's the secret.

So what about you? What can you do about it?

What have you tried so far?

> Avoiding danger is no safer in the long run than outright exposure. The fearful are caught as often as the bold.
>
> Helen Keller

You have probably already employed some strategies to counter fear. For example, have you already tried any or all of the following (which incidentally don't work)?

Avoiding all situations where you might be called upon to speak

This is a popular strategy though it does very little to help you avoid stress and pain. You turn down invitations to speak. Then your work situation increasingly demands that you *do* speak. So you prevaricate and postpone. You send members of your staff who don't mind speaking. You arrange presentations that involve your whole team with the excuse that you are making it a democratic event or providing a learning experience for them. You do this for as long as you can. But sooner or later you're up against some situation that is hard to avoid, and there you are back in the black hole of fear.

Beating yourself up

You tell yourself that you *should* be able to speak confidently. You tell yourself that you are a pathetic worm and that you will never amount to anything. You insist to yourself that you face your fears. You beat yourself up again and again. This all makes you feel very bad; beating yourself up never worked for anybody. So when you actually do speak in public your negative inner voice that has got so used to beating you up saps your confidence and sabotages your performance. The more you beat yourself up the worse you feel; and the worse you feel the more daunting the situation seems. It never works.

Telling yourself to be positive

You always think this should work. It never works. You tell yourself that you are feeling confident and that little voice pipes up inside you: 'Actually, I'm feeling really shaky.' So you revert to the previous strategy and beat yourself up verbally for a bit. Then you tell yourself again that you are feeling really positive; and the little voice pipes up a bit more stridently and wails, 'Hang on a minute. I'm feeling really bad, my knees are knocking.'

In fact, the more you tell yourself you are feeling positive the worse you get. You're not feeling positive at all. It's a lie.

Positive thinking is going to help you. But this isn't it.

Controlling the fear

We think that fear is our enemy and take steps to control it. We push the fear down and take a firm grip of ourselves both mentally and physically. Some people do this quite successfully: they stand up straight they keep their hands still. They do not quake; their voices are steady. You would guess that they weren't nervous. But they don't look nervous because they are dead. Well, not literally of course – but every bit of life has been squeezed out of their performance. The body is inert. The voice is flat and monotonous. The treatment of the subject even has that dull, impersonal, official quality as if they are reading a telephone directory. They never say, 'I have decided', they say instead, 'It has been decided'. They never say, 'I think it's a good idea', they say, 'It has been recommended that'. They have become robots. And robots outside science fiction lack

charisma, empathy, excitement, engagement, determination and every-thing else that makes us human and interesting.

As a strategy it doesn't work though people try it all the time! You could of course get by through using this method. But your audience deserves better, and so do you.

> A life lived in fear is a life half lived.
>
> Spanish proverb

How do effective speakers manage it?

We have already seen that successful communicators often get nervous and yet still produce great performances in spite of the fear (or could it even be *because* of the fear?). The important question is not, 'How do you get rid of fear?' but rather, 'How do you learn to perform so that fear doesn't inhibit your performance?' or even, 'How do you perform so that it *enhances* your performance?'

One actor found a way to stop himself getting nervous by desensitising himself to the point where he could go on stage and feel nothing. This enabled him to go on and play his part each night. But feeling nothing he just couldn't get his juices flowing and his performance always lacked spark. He discovered he didn't enjoy it any more. By getting rid of nerves altogether he lost something so important that acting no longer seemed worth doing.

The actor Judi Dench in an interview with Michael Parkinson confessed that she likes to feel fear:

> It's to do with free-falling and that's exactly what it is. I didn't realise – it's real fright. It's being pushed out of the plane ... I like to feel real fear. The more you [prepare for a script/role], the more is expected of you and the more frightened you get. *And the fear, like any emotion you feel, is what generates you.*[4]

So how can you get to such a point where nerves enhance your performance? Easier said than done? Some skills certainly seem easier to learn than others. Overcoming fear is not like learning how to solve cryptic crosswords or use a new gadget, where conscious application is effective. An emotion like fear does not respond readily to your conscious will. If you merely tell yourself not to feel nervous your conscious mind doesn't have much control over giving you the result you want. You stand at the podium determined to be confident; you launch into your speech and then despite yourself your knees start to shake. *Who told them to do that?*

Good luck charms

Whistling in the dark, our conscious mind gropes around for coping mechanisms. We make conditions, bargain with the gods or fall back on superstitions. Most of us are affected to a certain extent by circumstance when performing and our criteria for success can be detailed and particular:

- 'I can perform OK as long as I'm wearing my best suit or my red dress.'

- 'I'm fine as long as I don't know the audience.'

- 'I need to perform in front of friends.'

---

[4] *Parkinson*, 9 March 2002, BBC 1.

- 'I can perform to a few people but it can't be more than twenty.'

- 'I'm all right as long as there's no one too important in the audience.'

- 'I'm okay if I get up early enough, learn it off by heart and don't have to wait before speaking.'

- 'Things go well provided I've got my lucky horseshoe charm in my pocket.'

The beliefs we carry into performing situations can be pretty idiosyncratic.

Such thinking restricts you and keeps you scared. *Most importantly it puts the power on the outside*. The moment the numbers in your audience grow or someone important walks in your fear returns. It's out of your control. If you want to get the control back it is very important to take the next statement on board. You might not like it; you might not even believe it at the moment but it's this:

You create your own fear.

Fear is what happens in your head according to *how you react* to a situation. In other words, you do it to yourself. Olympic gold medallist and politician Sebastian Coe suggests, 'All pressure is self-inflicted. It's what you make of it or how you let it run off on you.'

How do you do fear?

If that is correct, and you inflict fear on yourself, then *how do you do it*? You can't beat it if you don't know how it works. So if I wanted to learn how to experience fear in exactly the same way as you what would I have to think, do, say or feel?

Making pictures and sounds

I asked a coaching client this question, and she replied: 'Well, first of all, if I am asked to give a presentation I want to know all about it and how much it matters. If I'm told that it's an important event, I instantly feel more nervous.'

'How do you do that?' I asked.

'Well, if my boss says it's an international event in a London hotel, I straight away think about how much he wants it to be a success and I start to imagine how he is going to be disappointed if it's not. I picture myself drying up on stage and see his face full of disappointment. I then hear him saying something withering like, "You let us down there, didn't you?" Then I feel terrible and begin to worry about how little I know and feel that I'm not sufficiently informed to speak on the topic.'

My client described one common strategy for creating fear – a very successful strategy as it happens if you *wanted* to create fear – and that is to create pictures of future disaster in your mind. She also added words and voices to the picture in her head which made it more compelling. Every time she returned to this catastrophic scenario she strengthened the connection between thinking about her presentation and pictures and sounds of disaster. This had been such a proficient learning strategy

that the connection had hardened into a habit and someone had only to suggest that she speak in public for her to go into panic mode by creating inner pictures and sounds that frightened her.

Making meaning

She made meaning of an event and the meaning scared her. Is this how you do fear? Think of some aspect of presenting that scares you and ask yourself what it is about it that worries you.

For example, if you tell yourself, 'I'm scared if there are more than ten people in the audience,' then ask yourself, 'What does more than ten people represent for me? What does it mean?' You might reply for instance, 'More than ten people means that I can no longer talk to them as individuals and this means that I am forced to perform or act and I feel that's something I can't do. It then becomes scary.' Or the meaning might be, 'If there are more than ten people they won't be close enough for me to use my normal speaking voice; therefore I won't be heard and they will get irritated and bored. That scares me.'

Going to future and past

Very often this process of making meaning takes you, as in the last example, into the future to imagine disaster. It can also take you into the past to remember disaster. It's usually a combination of the two with your negative past memories serving to amplify your fear of the future. If your boss is in the audience you may make meaning of it by instantly connecting this event with one that happened in your past. For example, 'The first time I spoke in front of someone with authority it was at primary school and the head teacher told me afterwards that I'd really embarrassed everyone and that I'd be much better not volunteering for such things in future.' The connection with such an event from distant childhood, even though so long ago, leaves you feeling infantile and hopeless and sabotages your present performance.

This is particularly toxic as there you are, living in the present, thinking and acting as an adult, but seeing your boss in the audience you suddenly become six years old. Not only do you feel small and vulnerable like a child, but the adult in you also feels critical and angry at yourself for appearing so pathetic. Your judgemental feeling *about* your feeling piles on an extra burden.

Generalising tragic thinking

Most of us have unhelpful stories from our past available and ready to connect instantly with present discomforts and impact negatively on our performance. Some of us regularly run through our repertoire of tragic tales and have one for every present circumstance:

'Tom didn't say hello this morning. I was always the one left out at school – what a sad sack I am!'

'I have just failed my driving test. I always fail everything. I even messed up learning to read.'

'Look, my hand is starting to shake. How pathetic is that? My ex-wife always called me a wimp; she was right to leave me.'

Some of us could win an award for our ability to prove ourselves inadequate time after time by producing a stream of life experiences to justify each present perceived failure. How much effort are you putting into proving a self-view of inadequacy? Did someone teach you how to do this? Most of us learned how to make these connections early in our life. Who was your model of how to do fear? Maybe it's time to update this early learning.

Change the connections

It's important to recognise that the associations you make in your head with impending future disaster or past disaster are *created by you*. Once you fully grasp the truth of this you can move on to the recovery stage, which is to understand that if you can make associations in this way, you can also learn how to make associations in a *different* way. In other words, you can choose to connect present situations with confidence-boosting experiences rather than self-sabotaging ones. You already know really well how to make connections. You just have to learn how to find more useful ones.

Your way of connecting your present situation with negative stuff is an old habit and it's time for change. Your subconscious which keeps the habit in place is like the Japanese soldiers who were discovered on a remote Pacific island in the 1970s still shooting at the enemy. They didn't realise that the war had ended twenty-five years previously. They were still in the habit of 'visitor equals enemy, therefore shoot!' Your subconscious – like the Japanese soldiers – will be delighted to be brought up to date.

Excellent speakers allow themselves to feel nervous but make meaning in a different way: 'Ah, I feel nervous. Yes, that's because this presentation really matters to me. I really want to do my best here. Of course I'm nervous. My nerves remind me that I want to prepare really well for this one.' Or 'The adrenaline's really coursing through me; I can't wait to get going.'

We will cover in detail later in this book how to create connections in your mind which, instead of sliding you towards despair, move you powerfully towards confidence and enjoyment.

The curse of perfection

> The person who never made a mistake never tried anything new.
>
> Albert Einstein

Just a few words on unhelpful beliefs before we embark on the success strategies. A particularly damaging belief for any kind of performance is the one that says, 'This must be perfect', and it comes with its evil twin, 'But I'm not good enough'.

The belief 'I'm not good enough' produces a host of unhelpful connections, such as, 'Mistakes are bad', 'I'm the only one who does this', 'There's something wrong with me', 'I'll never amount to anything', 'I can't perform', 'I'm stupid', 'I only got 98%, what happened to the other 2%?', 'What made me the dim-witted one of my family?'

Sound familiar?

Don't ever think about getting it right. Why? Because you're not going to get it right; how could anyone get communication right? And in any case it's not about getting it right – whatever 'it' is. Be happy with imperfection and then you'll create something excellent. Traditionally, every precious Persian carpet has at least one deliberate small fault in it. In that Middle Eastern culture only God is perfect so to weave a flawless rug would be to invite the evil eye.

What *is* perfection anyway? Once there was a man who gave a perfect speech; every word was practised and then uttered exactly as planned.

The arguments were carefully thought out; the choice of words was optimal. There was not a single mistake in the whole speech. The audience could not fault a single thing. But a small child huddled in the corner next to his father who had been unable to find a childminder commented, 'Dad, why is everyone asleep? Is it because the man is so boring?'

Success or failure thinking

> Success and failure – what is success anyway, a false idea. If we
> taught children to speak they'd never learn.
>> William Hull, quoted by John Holt in *How Children Fail*

Perfectionism is a fundamentalist approach, an example of black-or-white thinking: it's perfect or it's not. Another example of fundamentalism is success or failure thinking. We want our performance to be a success but we fear that it will result in failure; either/or – black/white. It's an approach that many of us learned as soon as we entered full-time education. A piece of work was correct or it had mistakes; a tick or a cross. Everything was judged a success or a failure, and the judge stood outside in the figure of the teacher or parent. That authority figure still lurks within us pronouncing each of our efforts a success or a failure.

This is particularly harmful thinking for any sort of performance and no great performer adopts this approach. As the educator John Holt says, 'There is no line with *Success* written on one side and *Failure* on the other. These words seriously distort our understanding of how we, as well as children, do things and do them better.'

When we even *think* in this way we tend to assume that it will be a personal disgrace if things don't go well. We take it all horribly personally, and every perceived specific failure is seen as a proof of our incompetence and lack of worth.

'I'm going to fail anyway'

> The greatest mistake you can make in life is to be continually
> fearing you will make one.
>> Elbert Hubbard, *The Note Book of Elbert Hubbard*

John Holt suggests that we sometimes deliberately cause failure to release unbearable tension. This explains why you may sometimes start a presentation well and then after a few minutes experience terrible feelings of fear which sabotage your performance. He explains with reference to his piano playing:

> As I play, the inner voice that comments on what I am doing says: 'All right so far; watch that G sharp; oops! narrow escape, you almost played F sharp instead of F natural, etc., etc.' The voice gets louder and louder, until finally the communication channels are clogged up, coordination breaks down, and I make the mistake I have been fearing to make … there is a peculiar kind of relief, a lessening of tension, when you make a mistake for when you make one, you no longer have to worry about whether you are going to make one.[5]

So forget success and failure – it really is not *about* that, and thinking in terms of making mistakes only leads to making them. The international violinist Nigel Kennedy writes in his autobiography about moving away from getting it right as a young violinist. He went through a period as a college student where during the day he obeyed his teacher and played as he was told, while at night he'd try different things out in front of a small audience. He found that by communicating his feelings rather than getting things 'right' everyone loved his playing.

For great performers there is no such thing as the perfect performance. Each individual time is different; each one is the way it is; each one is the creation of *this* time; each one is *this* one.

> Non, je ne regrette rien!
>
> Édith Piaf

New ways to learn

By understanding that it is about your thinking, it is possible to change the way you do things. You just need certain new elements in place.

The first thing to realise is that your conscious mind is not in charge of the show, so you need a new way to communicate with yourself. We have talked about the old way of telling yourself to be different and, however

---

[5] John Holt (1995). *How Children Fail*. Cambridge, MA: De Capo Press.

willing your mind is, it usually can't oblige. You say to yourself, 'Don't go *tight in the throat*' and your voice hears 'tight in the throat' and becomes constricted. You need to find a different way of communicating with the part of you that's getting in your way and you can do that through teaching your *body* what to do and by working on your beliefs, not by instructing yourself to feel different.

If you want to run a hundred metres within a certain time or perform any other strenuous activity with your body the first step is to get fit. For performing too you need a sound basis on which to build. Your success will depend on *how* you learn. Here are some learning principles based on the thinking of one of history's greatest geniuses, Leonardo da Vinci. Adopt these ways of thinking and you will make fast progress.

Leonardo da Vinci's way of learning

1. Be curious. No, be *very* curious. Don't worry about the outcome, just get wondering: 'That's fascinating ... why is that?'

2. Try things out. Don't just read this book – experiment. Find out what works and what doesn't ... *use* your curiosity!

3. Use all five senses. Often fear is based largely on one sense – for example, it is triggered by negative inner talk (sound) or by an internal picture of disaster (sight). Make use of every sense.

4. Welcome confusion – at least, don't be put off if you get confused. Every genuine breakthrough comes after a time of confusion. That's why it's a *breakthrough* not just a matter of slotting something into place. N.B. This may need a little patience!

5. Use your imagination *and* your ability to pay exquisite conscious attention to what is going on. You need both.

6. Learn in the muscle. Remember that your body – not just your brain – has to learn the new patterns. It's a bit slower than the mind so give it time.

7. Everything's connected and it will all come together when you're ready.

(Adapted from *How to Think Like Leonardo da Vinci* by Michael Gelb.[6])

It had long since come to my attention that people of accomplishment rarely sat back and let things happen to them. They went out and happened to things.

Leonardo da Vinci

---

[6] Michael J. Gelb (2000). *How to Think Like Leonardo Da Vinci: Seven Steps to Genius Every Day*. New York: Dell Publishing Co.

PART II

25 Confidence Strategies

CHAPTER 3

Use Your Imagination

Strategy 1 – Change fear to excitement

Let fear take you where you want to go!

> The birds of worry and care fly around your head. This you
> cannot prevent. But that they build a nest in your hair, this
> you can prevent.
>
> Old Chinese saying

So we're ready to go with the learning tools! We've talked about fear; let's look at what you need to do to handle it.

Don't think about fear.

What did you do when you read those words? For sure, you thought about fear!

Most of us put a lot of energy into struggling *not* to think about fear. We try to ignore our shaking fingers, our trembling legs, the knot in our stomach, the butterflies in our belly, the dizzy feeling in the head, the constricted feeling at the throat, the sweaty palms, the fast heartbeat and all the rest.

It's never successful because all our attention goes on *not* paying attention and the imagination cannot deal with negatives. If I tell you not to imagine a red double-decker bus what happens? Exactly – you think of a red double-decker bus! It is impossible not to. So if you tell yourself not to tremble your attention goes to trembling and you shake like a leaf. Moreover, you probably exaggerate the effect by going into the negative story-telling that we talked about before.

All this takes a lot of energy; and it's all energy wasted. None of the energy trapped into avoiding paying attention to what you don't want goes into giving a fantastic performance.

Don't use your energy to squash the fear. It's too difficult. And it's energy wasted.

Use your energy to go with the wave!

We give the name fear to a whole combination of symptoms – pounding heart, tight shoulders, shaking hands and so on – and then we feel bad about it. But what's in a name? Could you give the combination a different label instead? Could you call it for instance:

- a buzz?
- a rush?
- a high?
- get-up-and-go?
- being amped up?
- hitting the ground running?
- excitement?

Fear to excitement

Let's do some information gathering.

Remember how it feels to be nervous or afraid

Get to know that feeling. What is it for you? Butterflies? Sweaty palms? A knot in the stomach? Dry mouth? Feel again what it's like. Choose a genuine memory and observe and feel exactly what happens physically and mentally when you are nervous.

Then shake off the feeling

Get up and move around or think of something else – what you had for supper last night for instance.

Remember how it feels to be excited

Now recall a time when you were looking forward to some event with eager anticipation – like meeting someone you love after an interval apart or anticipating the next big descent on a fairground big dipper (if that's pleasurable for you!). Get to know that excited feeling. What is it like? Is it a bubbling feeling? Butterflies again? An upwards rush? Fast heartbeat? Observe and feel again what it is like.

Now transform fear into excitement

Enter fully again into the feeling of fear and gradually and elegantly change that nervous feeling into your feeling of excitement. Build up the sensation till you feel really excited.

Repeat the process a few times so that you become familiar with the sensation of changing fear into excitement.

Although for some individuals the two feelings are very different many people are surprised to find that the sensations are not a million miles apart. Maybe for you excitement has a more upward or outward feeling or you find that it allows you to breathe more fully. This is about your own experience.

Next time you feel afraid remind yourself that you are also excited and go through the process of changing the feeling of fear into the feeling of excitement. You may like to breathe in as you make the change and feel the upwards sensation that accompanies it.

You'll find that you feel more upbeat about the event and readier for action.

The psychotherapist Fritz Perls would tell people, 'When you're scared, just breathe a little and it'll turn to excitement.'

Most people find that going from a feeling of fear to a feeling of excitement demands a much smaller shift than attempting to change a feeling of terror into a feeling of calm. Thus it feels quite doable. Even telling yourself that the shaky feeling inside you is excitement rather than fear can change your attitude towards it.

Often, it really is just the difference of a name. Remember Bruce Springsteen? He reports that he is physically sick before every performance and then congratulates himself for getting excited. It's all in the *meaning* we make of our feelings. A feeling is just a feeling – an energy that is neither positive nor negative. It is only when we give the sensation the name of an emotion such as fear, excitement, worry or anticipation that it has the power to affect us for better or worse.

> Ultimately we know deeply that the other side of every fear there is a freedom.
>
> Marilyn Ferguson

Notes

People react differently to fear. Stella reported that as soon as she remembered a scary occasion she felt shaky all over. Stomach, knees, hands – everything trembled and her heart beat at a hundred times a minute. Then when she thought of something that excited her, the feeling was very similar; her stomach fluttered in anticipation, her heart beat fast and she felt quivery all over with an upward feeling as excitement rose in her chest. In fact the only appreciable difference between the two emotions was the upward feeling that caused her to take a breath. She laughed at the simplicity of it and realised that all she needed to do was call fear excitement in future and begin to enjoy the positive upwards sensation!

Martin on the other hand found that with fear everything went tight. There was a knot in the stomach and his throat closed up. He was unable to think clearly and felt blocked. He found it difficult to remember a feeling for excitement and therefore suspected that the strategy was not going to work for him. Staying with the thought of excitement he reflected that it made his heart beat faster and he remembered a vague feeling of looking forward to something. When he changed fear to excitement he was aware that the two feelings were different although he was unable to recall either of them very strongly. He sensed a greater sense of movement with excitement. He certainly reported that the feeling of excitement allowed him to take a better breath which felt positive. He thought that if he called fear excitement in future it would at least encourage him to breathe more fully.

Strategy 2 – Imagine what you want

Being a champion is not just a measure of your natural talent. It's a test of your ability to act and think like a champion. The more you act and think like a champion, the more of a champion you become.

Martin Perry, confidence coach and sports psychologist

Now you are ready to create your goal. The next strategy for overcoming performance anxiety is to imagine what you want.

Imagination might seem a rather flaky concept. Do not underestimate its power. The greatest successes of humans have happened because of someone's ability to *imagine*.

> I am enough of an artist to draw freely upon my imagination. Imagination is more important than knowledge. Knowledge is limited. Imagination encircles the world.
>
> Albert Einstein

> Imagination is powerful. Imagination is healing. All you need is the courage to visualise what should be, and then give yourself to its creation.
>
> Gabrielle Roth

> Imagination governs the world.
>
> Napoleon Bonaparte

> One supreme fact which I have discovered is that it is not willpower, but fantasy-imagination that creates. Imagination is the creative force. Imagination creates reality.
>
> Richard Wagner

Many of the highest achievers in sport use imagination to plan for winning. Bobsledders at the 2010 Winter Olympics visualised the entire run before they set out at the top. The legendary golfer Jack Nicklaus visualised the exact parabola that each ball would carve in the air before taking a shot.

Mihaly Csikszentmihalyi tells the story of a pilot who was imprisoned in North Vietnam for many years and became weak and emaciated in a jungle camp. After his release he requested a game of golf with other officers. To their great astonishment in spite of his condition he played an outstanding game. In answer to their enquiries he explained that every day during his imprisonment he had imagined himself playing eighteen holes, including every detail from choice of club for each shot to the systematic assessment of each hole in different conditions over different courses. His visualisations not only helped to preserve his sanity but had been as effective as physically practising each day.

This gives us a clue to how visualisation works. You see within your mind exactly what you want to take place. Your mind can activate success for the body or it can undermine it. Whatever you focus on in your mind creates neural pathways in your brain. So if you *want* success think about what that will look like, sound like and feel like. If you spend time thinking about failing you are conditioning your brain to look for difficulties – and it will find them.

It is important in using this strategy to go for what you want, not what you don't want. We are well conditioned through upbringing and schooling to be aware of what is not OK – for that is the gentle art of correction, the 'no' and 'don't' of parents and the red pen over pieces of school work. Maybe because of this conditioning many of us find it much easier to come up with what we *don't* want than what we *do* want:

'I don't want to look an idiot.'

'I don't want to show off.'

'I don't want people to think badly of me.'

and so on.

If this is what comes up first that's fine but you need to make what you want stronger than what you don't want, so make that clear in the words you use. Ask yourself, 'If I don't want to look an idiot, what do I want to look like?' Maybe you want to look credible or sure of yourself. In that case, put those words in your intention: 'I want to look credible and sure of myself' and then you can focus on something you are moving towards rather than away from.

Sometimes we think that we are focusing on what we want when we're not. We say for instance, 'I want to get through without messing up.'

Is that focusing on what we want? It starts with 'I want' after all. No, the clearest image is of 'messing up' – that is, of what I don't want.

It's important to realise that the subconscious doesn't understand negatives. If you say to yourself, 'Watch out or you'll spill that coffee,' in spite of the clear direction 'watch out' the subconscious also hears the words 'spill that coffee' as a command and ensures that you do spill the coffee!

This concept applies to all of the following:

'I want to avoid stumbling over my words.'
'Stumbling over my words' is what I don't want and what
I will actually get.

'I want to stop people feeling sorry for me.'
'People feeling sorry for me' is what I don't want and what
I will actually get.

'I want to feel less scared and worried.'
'Scared and worried' is what I don't want and what
I'll actually feel.

So express your wants entirely in terms of what you want to move towards:

'I want my presentation to be received with acclamation.'

'I want to be confident and enjoy connecting with Greg.'

Focus your attention entirely on *exactly* what you desire.

Energy flows where attention goes.

This statement can work for good or ill – you can visualise success or failure. A recent research finding in the *British Medical Journal* reported that old people who are anxious about falling and think about falling are statistically more likely to fall.[1] Fear makes the thing feared more likely to happen.

There is something about visualising success that can sound too good to be true to people. So they decide that it doesn't work. Don't believe them. That's just *fear*: fear of failure *and* fear of success. They are wrong: it works brilliantly. But only if you actually *do* it, however resistant you are, however stupid you feel and however much you can't believe it.

Just do it!

If you find that you don't see clearly in your mind's eye or you have difficulty in hearing sounds in your imagination, don't worry. Many people don't visualise clearly or hear remembered sounds distinctly – that doesn't matter at all. You just *do* it in whatever way you can. It gets easier and increasingly vivid the more that you practise it. And then it works! Your imagination is a wonderful tool. If you have ever imagined things going wrong when you think about public speaking and then discovered

---

[1] Kim Delbaere, Jacqueline Close, Henry Brodaty, Perminder Sachdev, and Stephen Lord (2010). Determinants of disparities between perceived and physiological risk of falling among elderly people: cohort study. *British Medical Journal* 341: c4165. Available at http://www.bmj.com/content/341/bmj.c4165.full.pdf (accessed 11 July 2011).

that they *did* indeed go wrong, you will know how effective your imagination can be! It might as well work *for* you and not *against* you!

Have a vision not clouded by fear.

Cherokee proverb

Imagine success

Imagine what success is going to look like, sound like and feel like.

Step into an imaginary scenario in which you are giving your speech. Imagine walking on with confidence and acknowledging your audience with warm friendliness. Imagine standing tall and confident, moving with ease and responding to questions with energy and humour. See what you would see if you were there looking out of your own eyes.

Hear yourself speak with assurance and power. Hear the absolute hush when you say something that has the audience hanging on your word. Hear the applause or positive response.

Feel yourself relax as you see their interested faces. Feel the warmth of being with a group that is aware of a connection with you. Feel the energy stream through you as you know that things are going well.

Again and again run over the desired scenario in your mind. Make it exactly the way *you* want it to be.

Not realistic? Keep your trust. Do it and do it again. Get to feel what it's like so that your body learns it. Then when you get to your live performance the pattern is set. Whatever your conscious mind gets up to your subconscious mind feels a familiarity with what it has practised and knows what to do.

Troubleshooting

I can't form pictures in my head or if I try they won't stay in one place.

Then start with whichever sense is strongest. Maybe for you it is easier to *feel* what it will be like to perform well. Get a sense of the physiology. How will you be standing? How will you hold your head? What feeling inside you represents confident energy? Some people find it easier to hear sounds than to form pictures. Hear the enthusiastic comments that people are making about your speech. Hear the excitement in the room as you speak. Hear your voice coming out strongly. Then you can add the visuals at the end. Don't worry if your image is not clear. Look for details in the picture to exercise your visual sense.

I try to see what I desire but keep finding that I'm drawn back to my current feelings and then the image disappears.

When you are practising the visual part of the exercise, instead of imagining that you are looking out of your own eyes you may prefer to imagine that you are looking at *yourself* on a film screen at quite a distance from yourself. Notice what difference that makes.

It's all very well but I can't do it because I just don't believe it.

Relax. You really don't have to believe it. Think of it as an exercise like warming up in the gym. It's the doing that matters at this stage, not whether it seems possible or not.

Strategy 3 – Play with the vision

> I have been visualizing myself every night for the past four years standing on the podium having the gold placed around my neck.
>
> Megan Jendrick, Olympic gold medallist in swimming

You can make your imagining more compelling by adjusting the qualities of the pictures and sounds you create until they are just as you would like them. Like a filmmaker you are completely in charge of the finished movie, so make it just as you would like it.

Adjust your TV set

You can do this exercise by yourself but it is particularly fun and effective to do with a friend. They can give you the instructions about changing the image and sounds leaving you free to concentrate on your inner world.

Imagine what you want as if you are looking at yourself on a cinema or television screen. Take your time to create the scene in your mind to make it as vivid as you can. You are going to make changes to the film, adjusting one aspect and then another in turn, to discover which changes make the film the most convincing and attractive.

If the picture is in black and white at first change it in your imagination to colour. Notice what difference that makes to how you respond to the image. Adjust the colours to make them more vivid. Then change them to pastel tones. Which do you prefer? Adjust the colours by making them lighter, darker, richer or more delicate until the picture looks really attractive. Give the picture sharp edges; now make them softer. Bring the image closer so that it is larger; now try it further away. Move the picture to your left, then to your right. What differences do the adjustments make? Take your time with each adjustment and notice the difference it makes to your feeling about it. Fine-tune the movie until it is really compelling and just as you would like it to be.

We have mentioned various different visual qualities you can adjust. Here are some other suggestions:

- Moving picture or still
- Bright, sparkling, faded or dim
- Opaque, translucent or transparent
- Three-dimensional or two-dimensional
- Action at normal speed, speeded up or slowed down
- Framed like a picture or a panoramic view

Now adjust the sounds of the film. Are they in stereo or mono or do they surround you? Are they coming from a particular direction? Alter these characteristics and see what difference they make. Is the sound coming from near or far? Adjust the volume, louder then softer. Make the sounds higher or lower in pitch and speed them up or slow them down. Give them an echo or muffle them. Make them as clear as a bell. Adjust the sounds until the event is utterly compelling and draws you into it.

Finally, step into your film as if you are there taking part in the scene looking out of your own eyes rather than looking at yourself in the picture. Experience what it is like to be acting in your own persuasive future. What are you feeling? You can also adjust those feelings. Give yourself more warmth or make the air fresher and cooler. If you are moving in your scene move with more energy and now move slower. Which do you prefer? Give your body lightness; now feel heavier and more grounded. Which gives you the better sensation? If you find that you want to adjust your physiology in the here and now to match the feelings then perhaps stand straighter, more relaxed or some other way. Maybe move around.

Make the whole experience as appealing as you can. Allow it to draw you in. Enjoy the experience of being in your ideal projected future and get to learn what it will be like to be there.

Isn't it good to know that you'll recognise it when it happens?[2]

Troubleshooting

I adjusted the size of the images and made them large but it felt overwhelming.

That's fine. Restore the images to the size they were in your mind originally or at least reduce them in size until it feels comfortable.

I thought brighter images would be best but they don't seem to be.

It's different for different people. You might like to make the images a pastel colour; some people find that more relaxing. Try also adjusting the tones to make them warmer or cooler. There is no right way – it's whatever appeals to you and you only discover that by experimenting.

I made the image sparkly and really liked it, but this isn't like real life.

It doesn't have to be; it's about making the image attractive so that it draws you in. A playful attitude works best. Try speeding the film up too; it's certainly not real life, but it can make everything seem less serious!

I just can't create images at all.

You can start with sounds instead; hear yourself speaking and listen to the sounds of the environment and other people. Then adjust the qualities of these.

---

[2] Developed by David Gordon (1978). *Therapeutic Metaphor: Helping Others Through the Looking Glass*. Capitola, CA: Meta Publications.

I don't know how to 'step into the film' – it seems to retreat from me and I'm still looking at myself in it.

Instead of stepping into the film allow the picture to wrap around you. Just put in all the images and scenery that would be around you.

I can't actually speak very loudly so there doesn't seem any point in raising the volume in my film. When I do this exercise I find myself feeling hopeless because in real life I'm not like this.

This isn't about what you can do in real life at present; it's about how the imagined changes affect you. Many people find that when they imagine a louder voice they feel stronger and more confident. And remember, if you wanted to run a marathon you wouldn't despair if you were unable to run 26 miles straight off on day one. You'd realise it was a journey of preparation. Be happy with whatever changes affect you positively; some will have more impact than others.

What's the point of feeling warmer or cooler; other people are not going to notice such changes?

Again, this is about the overall effect on you of making a particular change. You may find that feeling warmer makes you feel more courageous or at ease; increasing the feeling of lightness may release more energy; you won't know until you try it!

Strategy 4 – Find a good model

I worked a while ago with a young executive who was highly intelligent and had great aptitude for his work. But he had a particularly quiet voice and hated public speaking, so when he knew he had a conference coming up where he was required to speak he froze. We worked together to prepare for it but in spite of some improvement he continued to come across as stiff and subdued.

I asked him if he knew anyone who performed in a way he liked. He couldn't think of anyone immediately. Then he smiled, stopped smiling and said:

'No, I can't think of anyone.'

'So ... the smile?' I queried.

'Oh, that,' he confessed, 'I was just thinking of the guy from Santa Barbara.'

He explained that there was an executive who came over from time to time from one of their US companies and made everyone laugh all the time.

'How does he do it?' I asked.

'Well, he comes into the office, sits on one of the desks and just starts telling us about what's happening over there.'

'Show me,' I said.

'I'm not a bit like him,' he hedged.

'I quite understand. But what does he do?' I insisted.

The young executive got to his feet. After a couple of false starts he began to adopt a swagger and came across the room, perched himself on the edge of the table and began to talk in a strange accent. His voice came out clear and loud and his whole manner made me want to laugh.

'OK,' I said seriously, controlling my facial features with an effort. 'I can see that he's a bit different.'

The young executive laughed: 'It's amazing how he just has the confidence to be like that. I'd love to be like that.'

'What? Like you have just shown me?'

'Yes! Like I've ...'

There was a pause of recognition. 'Ah. I've just done it, haven't I?'

'Yup, you've just done it.'

It is extraordinary how we are held back from doing things by our limited self-image. If we imagine that we are someone else we begin to be able to do what they can do. It's all made up: we don't actually become someone else. But we do possess the ability to imagine ourselves in a different way and that imagination is the means to get a more wide-ranging view of what's possible for you.

The actor Jane Horrocks was required to sing like Marilyn Monroe in the film *Little Voice* yet she confessed that in ordinary life she didn't have the voice to achieve it:

> My own singing voice is not very good ... When I think of Marilyn Monroe, and achieving her sound, I think of having a rather large bust. I think of her physically and I am just able

to create her sound, because her physicality was so much to do with her sound. It was such a breathy, pouty, sexual thing that unless you are thinking of it I think it is hard to create her ... I just find it thrilling, especially when I totally lock into the person that I am doing and I'm really flying.[3]

So you can expand your ability to perform well by finding a model and experimenting with it.

Modelling good communicators

Think of someone you admire as a communicator. It might be someone you see and hear on television, a comedian or an anchor for instance. It might be someone you know personally, a friend you chat with in the pub or someone from work. It could even be someone you have read about or a famous figure from history.

So, pretend to *be* that person. Stand and walk as you imagine they do, gesture in the same manner, make similar facial expressions. Use your voice the way they do. Don't hold back in any way; just enjoy being them and getting the feel of what they do. See this as a child's game. You don't have to get it right. You don't have to be authentic. You don't have to achieve a specific objective. This is for its own sake, just for fun to see what happens.

What now becomes possible in your new persona? Isn't it amazing? You can actually do anything if *you* don't hold *you* back!

Case study

Kerry chose the prize-winning author Arundhati Roy whom she had heard on the radio and liked for her mixture of gentleness and inner firmness. She found it hard to speak like her at first and decided to ignore the Indian accent as she began to speak about justice in Kashmir. She discovered a stillness in herself which quite surprised

---

[3] See http://www.bbc.co.uk/worldservice/arts/highlights/001027_horrocks.shtml, 27 October 2000 (accessed 11 July 2011).

her. She stood tall and relaxed, head high and spoke gently, but her voice was clearly audible. She felt calm, convincing and strong. She reported that the feeling was profoundly different from her normal way and allowed her to feel more peaceful and centred.

Gavin chose the young comedian Russell Howard as he liked his high energy and humour, but he felt self-conscious and struggled when he pretended to be him. Then he suddenly remembered how the comedian runs onto the stage so he threw caution to the winds and tried that. Instantly, with the increase of adrenaline he caught a flavour of his dialogue and surprised himself with the energy he demonstrated. After an excellent portrayal the experiment ended with him breaking down laughing. He found the experience quite liberating.

Strategy 5 – Transfer an ability

I used to work sometimes with a good friend who got very nervous about presenting. Marion was a brilliant consultant who advised companies and helped chief executives and teams to improve their business. It was just presenting that she hated. Sometimes when she had a presentation coming up she would phone me and ask for help in writing her speech. Then we would go through in great detail what she was going to say and how she was going to say it. She still got very nervous and her voice used to become soft and breathy as soon as she spoke in public. This happened every time.

One day, she was asked at very short notice to facilitate a meeting including discussion on how to improve communication. She was told that the people in the meeting lacked clarity about what to do. She collected a few ideas together in her mind and went along. In fact, no one at the meeting had any idea whatsoever how to proceed so she spoke to them for forty-five minutes or so. They were delighted with her ideas and the meeting went really well.

When she told me about the occasion, I said to her, 'Marion, that was presenting.'

'What do you mean, that was presenting? I don't *do* presenting. I was just talking to the group about their issue.'

'Exactly; it's called presenting.'

'Oh. I thought you had to *perform* when you present. I'm no actor and that's why I hate it.'

'Well, call it something different then!'

'I think I will!'

Very often, we find something scary because we put it in a particular mental box. Marion put her scary stuff in a box called 'presenting'.

When I work with people in organisations I come upon this very often. Many people think that there is an established list of criteria for making a presentation and that it contains all the things that they find awkward or difficult, like knowing everything, looking superior to everyone, following a strict code in the use of PowerPoint slides and commentary and performing like an actor. Not so.

Presenting is just communication – and you have been communicating all your life.

A piano tutor from one of the London music colleges told me the story of one of her pianists, a borderline student who struggled at every stage in college to make the grade. As the final examinations drew near the student became less and less competent. In particular, she had a real problem with memorising her pieces, an essential accomplishment for the final recital. She got to a point where she was unable to remember even short sections in her lesson. The tutor tried everything without success. Finally, when all her regular strategies had failed she decided to think laterally.

She asked the student what she felt like on college mornings. The student replied that since her first arrival at the London college three years before, every morning the moment she arrived at the top of the steps from the underground station she felt physically sick with anxiety. What a burden of feeling to bring into college each day!

The tutor asked her questions to find some area of her life where she felt confident and discovered that she ran an amateur musical theatre group which she loved. When she was conducting that she felt sure of herself, happy and in control.

The tutor asked her to remember such an occasion and feel again strongly that wonderful self-assured feeling she had when conducting her group. The student was able to do it with ease. They worked on accessing and maintaining the feeling. 'Now,' said the tutor, 'feel again that feeling and play to me.' The effect was instantaneous. Her playing improved dramatically that very day and in that new state of mind her ability to remember improved as well. After more work she took the final examination, played from memory and passed with excellent grades.

Transfer an ability from a different context

Find a context in which you are comfortable communicating with more than one person at a time. Maybe it's when you eat out with a group of friends or when you entertain people at home; maybe it's at a social event with colleagues; perhaps it's when you have a group of children in the house or when you are with your family.

Remember what it's like to communicate with people in that context.

- How do you move and speak?
- What kind of thoughts go through your head?
- What does it feel like?

Then forget the word 'presentation' or 'speech' and remember that giving a presentation is just what you do in the more comfortable context: it's just communicating.

I can hear some objections coming up: 'Yes, but I'm not scared then. In any case, there's nothing special about those times to remember. It's just different.'

Yes, that's the point. It's just different. Capture that difference. It takes only a little of that to rub off onto your presentation style to make a positive impact – something about your sense of ease, how you hold your body, your interest in other people – what is it?

Get really curious about what you do in those situations where you feel comfortable. Get used to feeling that sensation. Then transfer the feeling to the time when you speak in public. If you get to know the sensation well you'll be able to find it again when you need it.

Case study

Stephen was troubled that he could not think of a single example of a time when he felt comfortable communicating with a group. He could think of occasions when he had comfortable conversations with a good friend, but he wasn't able to remember any particular feelings he experienced in that context. He reported that one-to-one it all felt natural and that he had nothing particular to say about it. When pressed, he admitted that 'natural' included being relaxed, breathing easily and feeling 'okay'.

When invited to include those elements in talking to a group it suddenly came home to him how tense he was. He then realised that when he let go of tension and continued to breathe it made him feel friendlier towards his audience and he liked that. It also made him realise that he usually thought of a presentation as some sort of battle, and he decided to set that thought aside and concentrate instead on feeling at ease.

Strategy 6 – Think about after the ball is over

Time does not stand still. Every time you get anxious about something the moment eventually arrives when it is all over and you don't feel anxious any more. Being anxious is always about the future; you get anxious about something that has not yet happened. Once it has happened – whatever the outcome – that particular feeling goes away.

This strategy is about focusing on how you are going to feel when your challenge is over. This focus on a future feeling can utterly change your connection with the present moment.

Focus on afterwards

Think of a speaking challenge coming up. Let your mind travel forward to the time when you have completed the event. It is all over and you are feeling relieved and pleased that it has gone really well, that you did everything you wanted to and have had an excellent reception. Breathe out with all the relief of letting go of tension after the event. Feel the pleasure of a job well done. How satisfying to know that all has gone well. How good to breathe deeply again feeling content after the event.

Think about what you are going to do now that it is over. Are you going to chat with friends about how motivating it feels to have got through the challenge so well? Are you going to laugh with someone about how wonderful it is now to relax and let go? Are you going to have a comforting bath or shower, something nice to eat or drink or a bit of time off? Are you mentally brushing your hands together to signify that the job is finished and thinking forward to the next thing on your agenda? Breathe out again in a warm comfortable sigh – good to feel you've done what you set out to do!

Case study

Martin thought about a challenge coming up for him and then attempted to think about after the event, but however much he tried all he could come up with was worry about the challenge, and he confessed that he had no idea how to 'feel' something that had not yet happened. He could however remember feeling good after events in his past. In particular he remembered the wonderful sensation of 'walking on air' after a nerve-wracking degree ceremony.

When asked to relive that feeling he had no problem and found himself punching the air in triumph as he had done back then, certificate in hand, after the ceremony. He then took that energetic feeling into the upcoming challenging situation in his mind and, as he remembered the 'walking on air', he realised that it did indeed give him confidence that he would see the situation through. He remarked afterwards that 'treading lightly' – i.e. not being so serious about everything – was a really helpful thought for him to use when presenting.

This section has been about going for what you want. Now it is very likely that some part of you refuses to believe that it will work. But recognise this truth. Even as you acknowledge that you get scared – that sometimes you don't feel good enough, that you're not comfortable and all the other feelings that get in your way – if you just allow yourself to focus on what you want you will find miracles begin to happen for you.

It really is that easy.

CHAPTER 4

Be Present

> When you make friends with the present moment, you feel at
> home no matter where you are.
>
> Eckhart Tolle

So now we come to you as presenter; not what you do or don't do or what you say or don't say, but how you are in yourself. Great presenters have a wonderful ability to be at ease in their own skin in any situation and through being themselves they are able to make their audience feel comfortable and engaged.

When you are scared you get self-conscious and this separates you from your audience. So how can you get rid of this self-consciousness to allow your real self to shine through?

By staying in the present.

Strategy 7 – Focus externally

Look outward

What does it mean to be self-conscious? The expression explains it: you are conscious of self and thus aware of internal thinking and feeling, often experienced as an internal voice. Your inner critical voice can be a harmful gremlin in public speaking, creating havoc for you with its endless monologue. You may also notice that the internal talking is frenetic and slightly hysterical in character and affects your state of mind. The next strategy for dealing with fear provides a secure place where the gremlin cannot knock you off balance with its negative stuff. And where is that place? It's the *present*.

You'll probably be surprised to learn that when you are nervous and feeling all the discomfort of the present situation you spend almost no time at all in the present. Instead you go continually to the future and the

past, and use this time travel to make yourself feel bad. Your gremlin inner voice – that incessant chatter in the head – is really good at it. For example:

Future: 'You know the CEO is coming? That'll put the pressure on. People in your position shouldn't be nervous. He's very critical if you stumble over your words. You'll just have to make sure you don't stutter. I don't know what he'll say if you do. I know he's dropping hints about promoting you but it'll never happen if he discovers you can't even give a speech confidently. Imagine a member of the senior management team who can't present to the board! You might even trip now going up to the podium. You'll make a real idiot of yourself if that happens ...'

Past: 'Remember you did fall over once – it was that long cloak you had to wear as one of the three kings in the school nativity play. Oh, that certainly made everyone laugh at you! Mrs Williams got quite cross too: she said it was the last time she'd allow you a major part in a play – it made you really nervous when you read in class after that. She was right – you were hopeless. Everyone made fun of your Welsh accent too. Good idea for someone like you to avoid the limelight ...'

Future: 'But I've got to do this in a minute, and the CEO is coming, oh dear ...'

That gremlin can take you to a depressing place with its endless supply of negative stories! It's pretty persistent and locks your thoughts inside yourself. The only way to stop it is to replace it with something else. You cannot pay attention to your inner thoughts and feelings and to the external world *at the same time*, so one way not to get stuck inside with the gremlin is to focus on the world outside. It's about staying with what is in the here and now in an entirely literal way.

External focus

This is very easy: you just have to notice what's in front of you. Stand as if you are about to speak in a situation you might find challenging and do the following.

First, use your eyes

See the room, see the walls, the marks on the walls, the ceiling, the lights and the light fittings; see the floor and the patterns of the floor surface. Focus on what is actually there in front of you. Run through all the things you can see like an inventory in your mind. As you see each object say its name in your mind, 'There's the light in the ceiling. It has a red shade. The walls are cream ...'

Then use your ears

Hear the sounds in the room, the central heating, the buzz of people, traffic in the street, birds outside and the noise of feet on the pavement. Distinguish the differences in the sounds – which are near and which are far away, which are high pitched and which low. Run an inventory of these in your mind too.

Use your sense of touch and external feeling

Feel your feet inside your shoes; feel their weight in contact with the floor; feel your hands touch your clothes. Notice your breath as it goes in and out of your nose – in and out, in and out. No stories, no meanings – just notice, and speak what you notice inside your head if you want: 'I can feel the cool air pass up my nose. My socks feel soft in my shoes ...'

It's important in this exercise to make sure that you carry out the process without making *meaning* of what you notice. Whatever you see and hear is physical and whatever you feel is a bodily sense of touch not the name of an emotion.

Bonus thought

Having directed your thoughts so far you can usefully go one step further. It is sometimes said that if you tell people three true things they will believe whatever you tell them next. So try this out on yourself: after three true external observations – something you see, something you hear and something you feel or touch – add an affirmation as a fourth thought at the end like this:

1. I see the tall windows
2. I hear the traffic outside
3. I feel my toes in my shoes
4. And I'm enjoying feeling in control.

Your fourth thought can be any statement you choose that will make the event more satisfying and successful for you. For example:

- And I'm feeling comfortable and relaxed.
- And I'm really looking forward to this session.
- And I'm feeling energised and ready for anything.
- And I'm enjoying the feeling of connection with people.

After three true statements it becomes very easy to believe the truth of the fourth.

Use peripheral vision

You hear about speakers having 'presence'. You may have captured a sense of this presence in certain speakers yourself. Presence is in essence very simple. You just have to be *present* and aware in the moment – and this is just what you have being doing in noticing externally. By being present you are in the here and now, not thinking about past disasters or future fears of failure or judgement, but just being in the moment second by second by second.

In the present you will be aware of your surroundings through 180 degrees. Your peripheral vision at the edges of your visual field is particularly aware of movement and picks up a clear sense of the atmosphere of the present moment.

Peripheral vision

Lift your arms in front of you to the horizontal and stretch them out sideways to the right and left. Wriggle your fingers. Keep your head facing forwards and with your peripheral vision notice to what extent you can be aware of the movement of your right and left hands at the same time. If you are not aware of the movement move your hands forward just a little until you are aware of both.

Have a sense of the space around you, and be aware of whatever is moving in that space. Movement gives you a good indicator of the state of your audience. When people are very still it is usually a sign that they are intent on what you are saying (or entirely asleep!). When they become fidgety this is usually a sign that they are getting restless or losing interest and need something different from you. Capture the moment.

Case study

Sometimes a strategy seems just too simplistic. Rachael confessed that the idea of external focus irritated her. She couldn't see how something so elementary could be useful. However, it was explained to her that as humans find it impossible to focus the mind on nothing the mind has to be somewhere, and if not given something to do it will resort to its own stories. She was asked more than once, 'Where is your mind focused now?' After prevaricating a bit, she confessed that her mind was indeed focused on her discomfort and feeling of stress. 'So focus on something different.'

When she overcame her resistance and actually did the exercise as described she realised that its elementary nature did not in fact matter; that *anything* that took her mind out of its circular worrying pattern could be useful.

At this moment she suddenly had a realisation. 'Ah, that's why it's so simplistic – I don't *want* to be thinking about anything complex at this point – I have a speech to deliver after all! This is a just a strategy to avoid my own negative commentary. I get it!'

She confessed later that feeling her toes in her shoes had the additional benefit of balancing and grounding her in the present moment. From then on this became an important part of her regular preparation before speaking.

Strategy 8 – Find 'the zone'

This now is it. Your deepest need and desire
Is satisfied by this moment's energy
Here in your hand.

Rumi

When you are completely present in the here and now and fully focused on the task in hand you can enter a state called 'flow' – also known as being 'in the zone' by sports people or 'in the groove' by music people. In this state, your concentration is sharp, everything becomes easy and you just know that everything is going wonderfully well.

There are many examples from the fields of sports, arts and science. The Formula One driver Ayrton Senna described his experience when he broke all records in his qualifying round for the 1988 Monaco Grand Prix: 'Suddenly I was nearly two seconds faster than anybody else … and I realised that I was no longer driving the car consciously. I was driving it by a kind of instinct, only I was in a different dimension.'

Research by Jessica Witt, a psychologist at Purdue University in Indianapolis, revealed that golf players who are playing well see the hole as bigger than people who are playing less well. She suggests therefore that perception affects performance – and maybe vice versa.[1]

Now, you may feel that you are a long way from performing in the zone. You may just be hoping that you can make it through to the end without worrying about being in the zone or not; but the idea of being in flow has something to teach us about a state of being that is going to work well for you and show you the path to success.

Being in the zone is about being pleasantly relaxed *and* energised at the same time. Relaxed is not the same as being slumped, as when you watch TV on an evening when you're feeling exhausted. It means that your body is pleasantly free of tension but awake. Energised is not the same as being wired up, nervous or hyper. It means that you feel optimistic and

---

[1] Witt, J.K., Linkenauger, S.A., Bakdash, J.Z. and Proffitt, D.R. (2008). Putting to a bigger hole: Golf performance relates to perceived size. *Psychonomic Bulletin and Review*, 15, 581–585.

full of get-up-and-go. When you put these two frames of mind *together* you end up with a powerful state that feels both spontaneous and joyful. It's a state martial arts practitioners practise constantly: it requires you to be calm and ready at the same time; it's a state that allows you to make crucial split-second decisions each moment with unerring judgement while remaining unruffled.

Entering into the zone

To discover this powerful state for yourself think of a time when you were happy, relaxed and energetic at the same time. You were absorbed with whatever activity you were engaged in and your body was not putting up any resistance. It will be an occasion when you were having a really good time and therefore felt happy and relaxed but were also doing something which fired you up with an inner energy.

Some examples for you might be:

- Dancing

- Going on an exhilarating ride at a theme park

- Feeling the wonderful buzz of a close conversation

- Engaging in some pleasurable activity in good company

- Enjoying your own physical prowess as you took part in some sport for your own pleasure

What you are looking for in remembering such a time is *what it felt like* in your own skin to be relaxed and happy and at the same time energised and awake.

When you have found an example, relive the experience in your mind; see the event, hear its sounds, feel the great feeling you had at the time. Enjoy it fully.

This is the perfect state of mind for giving an amazing performance. Go back to your memory of this state of mind frequently and get to know it well. Experiment with various examples of it in your life. Remember what it feels like – in your body, in your head, in your heart and spirit. Remember so frequently that you can return to the state at will. It's a precious resource.

Troubleshooting Conversation

I don't think I've ever had an 'in the zone' experience – certainly not with other people.

What about on your own?

You mention sport and I do mountain climbing, but though I find it exhilarating it terrifies me.

What's it like?

Well, when I'm climbing sometimes it's incredibly scary and I almost feel I can't do it. But when I do – even though it feels like life and death – I get an amazing feeling of adrenaline that gives me a real high. It's as if I might die at any moment, yet I'm grinning! I'm actually not thinking about anything at all apart from the job in hand; I'm just caught up in the intense moment.

That's exactly it. That's the feeling you take into a presentation.

That's crazy; it's dangerous and risky and I'm scared ... Oh, I get it – it's also electrifyingly alive! I suppose if I can do that I can do anything – if I trust it.

Yes, with trust you can do anything.

Strategy 9 – Use association triggers

Association triggers are a grand way of describing what happened with Pavlov's dogs. Do you remember the Russian doctor Ivan Pavlov? He ran an experiment using a bell to call dogs to their food and after a few repetitions the dogs began to associate the bell with the promise of food and started to salivate in response to the bell not just in response to the food. The bell triggered a conditional reflex.

In the last exercise you remembered a time when you were in flow, relaxed and energised at the same time. Now you want a way to be able to enter that state at the time you need it – including when you perform in public. An effective way to achieve this is to invent your own equivalent of Pavlov's bell by finding some signal or trigger that you will learn to connect with the state you want. This is not a new concept; we use association triggers to change our state all the time though we might not call them that – for example, when we put on a soothing piece of music to get into a calm frame of mind or when we switch on a television comedy show to lighten our mood.

If you are to use this as a strategy when giving a presentation, you will want your equivalent of Pavlov's bell to be silent and invisible so that you don't draw people's attention to it. Performers using this strategy sometimes use an insignificant finger gesture that means something to them but is not easily noticed by others: for example, you may like to touch your little finger with your thumb or pinch a finger with your thumbnail as your reminder of the wanted state.

This trigger strategy will be familiar to many successful sports people who use it to remind them of the highly focused, balanced state of mind they have been cultivating in practice.

Fire the 'in the zone' trigger

To make the connection between the stimulus (trigger) and the action (being in the zone) recall a time in any context when you were in flow and everything seemed effortless and enjoyable (as you did in the last strategy). See what you were seeing at the time, hear what you were hearing and feel what you were feeling. When the sensation is at its optimum, touch your little finger with your thumb (or activate whatever trigger you have chosen).

You can also take examples of times when you were in other good states – e.g. focused, happy, confident or at ease – and follow the same process. Relive the feeling and use the same trigger to bring back the feeling when you want it.

Take your mind forward to a challenging situation and 'fire' your trigger to enter the desired state. Notice how the trigger summons up the state.

The next time you give a presentation or embark on some challenging event gently touch your little finger and thumb together before you speak or act and trigger your memories of being in the zone. Feel that power surge into you.

Practise your association triggers frequently. You will find it gets easier and quicker to access the state you want the more you practise.

Troubleshooting

I can recall times when I've been in flow and everything seemed effortless but I haven't the least idea how to capture it. It's just history for me.

It's possible that you are remembering it but not feeling it. If you are seeing yourself in your mental picture you are not actually reliving the past time; you are as it were just watching a film of yourself. The trick is to float back to that time in your mind and relive the experience with all the feelings and bodily sensations you experienced at that time – just as if you are no longer in the here and now but are actually back in that time living in it as in the present, seeing what you see, hearing what you hear and – most importantly – feeling what you feel.

Surely I need a different 'trigger' for each of my good feelings?

Well, you *could* do that, but it isn't necessary. If you use the same trigger you will find that the good feelings stack up one on another and give you a resourceful state that makes you feel ready for anything!

I'm not sure I need this finger trigger. As soon as I remember being in flow I'm straight away in that state feeling good.

That's just great. Use whatever works for you.

Strategy 10 – Centre yourself four ways

> With the past, I have nothing to do; nor with the future. I live now.
>
> Ralph Waldo Emerson

Now we look at ways to find your calm centre. When you are present you have an oasis of calm inside you and an acute awareness of everything that is going on. The ability to find this state can be immensely useful to you in challenging situations to help you stay focused or to regain your sense of calm if you become flustered.

The martial art of aikido offers four different methods to access the state of being present in the moment. You can bring one or another of the methods into your consciousness according to different circumstances. You will find that in some contexts one method will work most strongly and in others another will be more powerful. The different ways seem almost mirror opposites of each other yet each will take you to that calm centre in the eye of the storm. In aikido they are sometimes described as the four rules of mind and body coordination. In each of the four you are both relaxed and ready for action.

1. Keep one-point – 'focus ki'

To find your strong, calm centre stand tall and relaxed, shoulders loose, knees soft and back elastic and wide. Now focus your attention on a point about 5 cm below the navel, which roughly corresponds with the body's centre of gravity. Sense your focus there like a powerful light or a golden ball that rests in the same place in your body and moves as you move. Feel the light growing brighter and stronger as you focus on that place. This is a mental exercise where you create an image in your mind of the energy in your centre.

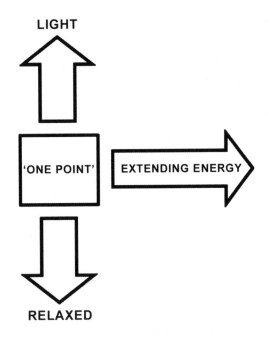

2. Extending energy – 'extend ki'

Stand as before. Raise one arm straight in front of you horizontally at the level of your shoulders pointing ahead. Imagine that your arm is a lightsaber with a powerful beam that extends out in front of you from the tips of your fingers into the distance. Maintain the sensation of a very bright light, and feel its energy spreading out beyond you powerfully. This also is a mental exercise where you create the image of the powerful beam of light in your mind and feel its energy extend beyond you. Alternatively, you can think of the energy extending from your fingers like a powerful water-hose.

3. Relaxed – 'be at complete ease'

Stand as before. Eliminate all unnecessary tension without going limp. This will induce in you a state of calm where you are awake and ready for action. If you like, you could imagine yourself as a large rock in a river. However much the water rushes over and past you, you remain heavy and immovable. This is a body feeling of heaviness, the heaviness of accepting, releasing, freeing and letting go, not giving up.

4. Light – 'keep weight underside'

Feel the lightness of your body. This gives your body a dynamic feeling of relaxation. Feel the weight on the underside of your feet and limbs and the lightness above. This also is a body feeling: as you feel the weight on the underside of feet, arms and shoulders, you are also aware of lightness on the upper side, giving you the sensation of nimbleness, grace and energy.

Practise these four ways of centring until you find it easy to centre in each of them. You can practise anywhere – in a quiet place or in the midst of a crowd. The calm-but-ready state of martial artists is a great state for anyone wanting to perform at their best for any occasion.

Notes

Each of the methods will help you to feel calm and centred and they are interchangeable. However, they are different and you will get more from the exercise if you begin to appreciate the differences. People often find that while one way of centring comes naturally another feels more difficult. This can be because this kind of energy has been neglected in the past. Perhaps you have been able to feel strong and centred but haven't realised that lightness is invaluable too. Or you have been able to find a sense of calm inside but have never realised the strength that can accompany it.

Remember in each case to remain awake and alert; it is never about giving up or slumping. Be aware that at any moment you could spring into action; yet you are still and centred, and your breathing is calm. You are like a cat poised to spring; your stillness is no effort and you could remain still for a long time; but your whole body expresses readiness.

This exercise takes no more than a few minutes. Doing one centring after another brings out the subtle differences and intensifies the effect. After working with this exercise for a while people sometimes comment that now for the first time they know what it feels like to be together, all of a piece.

CHAPTER 5

Come Alive

Strategy 11 – Use energy before you start

> People say that what we're all seeking is [*sic*] a meaning for
> life. I don't think that's what we're really seeking. I think what
> we're seeking is an experience of being alive, so that our life
> experiences on the purely physical plane will have resonances
> within our own innermost being and reality, so that we actu-
> ally feel the rapture of being alive.
>
> Joseph Campbell

I once watched a television programme about a celebrated event where
the three most famous operatic tenors in the world came together to
sing in a joint concert in Rome. With the strong competitive element
engendered it was a high pressure event even for artists who were used
to performing to huge audiences all over the world.

In one scene in the programme the singer Plácido Domingo is seen
pacing up and down quite fast in the wings wringing his hands vigorously
together as if highly nervous. He then pauses, takes a slow, immense
breath and seems to grow larger before our eyes. As soon as he has taken
the breath he walks purposefully onto the stage with every appearance
of supreme confidence. He stands before the vast audience, opens his
mouth and his glorious sound issues forth.

He used a strategy to prepare for his entrance that will work for you
too: he expended energy before he started. When you are nervous
the adrenaline you produce is liable to poison your system and block
your flow. So the answer is to use plenty of well-directed energy *before*
the event to get rid of the adrenaline and be ready to hit the ground
running.

Physical energy preparation

Try any or all of the following and sense how alive and ready for action you feel.

- Go for an energetic walk or run beforehand to get the energy flowing.

- Move on the spot or jump up and down.

- Shake your shoulders and stretch in all directions.

- Screw your toes up tightly inside your shoes and stretch them out again.

- Make tight fists with your hands under the table and then stretch the fingers out.

- Move your facial muscles vigorously.

- Breathe out strongly and take in fresh air.

- With your arms by your sides shake your hands and wrists vigorously for a few seconds as if you are trying to shake drops of water from them; then for a few more seconds shake them just as vigorously but with half the movement; and then just as vigorously but with half the movement again; and then half again and half again until the movement is tiny but the energy huge. Then stand still and feel the confident energy in your fingertips and throughout your body.

Now, having practised one or more of the energisers above, put your head up and your shoulders back and practise 'walking on'. As the energy floods through you step briskly onto your stage. Stand for a moment facing your audience, aware of this energy still running through your body. With that same energy announce yourself using your own words in a lively voice; for example:

'Good morning everyone! My name is Judy Apps and I am going to talk to you today about Iceland's powerful, active geysers.'

It will be easy for your audience to respond positively to that energy.

Notes

When physical activity is involved it's easy to work too hard at it. This exercise is not the same as going to the gym – you don't have to put lots of effort into it. If you can do the energetic movements with a friend and have a laugh about it at the same time that will probably have the best effect! It's just about coming alive.

When you have completed an exercise, pause for a moment and stay still to feel the energising effect through your whole body.

When you 'walk on' to introduce yourself, again don't work hard at it; it doesn't have to be polished or perfect. Just focus on the energy you have created and enjoy using its tingling power. Walk purposefully, speak energetically and enjoy it – no holding back!

On occasions where you do not have the opportunity to move from your seat before speaking, use an 'invisible' energiser such as screwing your toes up in your shoes.

Strategy 12 – Ride your fear like the rapids!

This sounds dangerous – but not as dangerous as standing still and being eaten alive! Some fear responses work better than others and riding your fear like the rapids works really well.

You may have read about the stress responses of our ancestors. Caveman wanders in the forest. Grizzly bear appears. Caveman responds in one of two ways: he attacks the bear or he runs away. Fight or flight. There is also a third option more often chosen by a rabbit in headlights than a caveman: he *freezes* in the hope that the bear won't notice him or just to pretend that it isn't happening.

The same choices apply to us in dangerous – read 'stressful' – situations today. The boss asks for the impossible. We can choose to fight – verbally maybe. We can leave the room in a hurry – flight. Or we can swallow the negative emotions we are feeling and act as if everything is fine (meanwhile building up the stress levels inside). Neither fight nor flight fit too well in today's workplace so the third option is the one most often taken; and for many this choice of response becomes a chronic habit. Freezing often seems like a good idea in the short term but it is a particularly inhibiting reaction as it closes down possibilities for action and leaves us feeling stuck and helpless.

When people get nervous before performing they have similar choices.

Fight
Fear leads some people to treat the audience as if it is the enemy. For others nerves can make them appear hostile when they are not; they put

on the armour to protect themselves and come across like angry warri-
ors, aggressive in tone and gesture. Some think of ways to get the better
of the audience. They invent strategies to cut the audience to size like
pretending that everyone is naked. They work themselves up into a fury
before presenting and then present a fighting persona, embodying the
belief that 'attack is the best form of defence'.

Freeze

When fearful some people freeze on stage; we've discussed them before.
They grip the podium, stand like ramrods and speak with a flat, mono-
tone voice. Their stomach ties in a knot, their throat constricts and their
mouth goes dry. They act like robots. In the worst cases they behave like
a rabbit in the headlights: the brain goes blank and they no longer know
what they are doing or where they are.

Flight

Some people have the instinct to flee as soon as they begin to speak. The
instinct comes out in rushed speech and the inability to keep still. They
pace up and down or rock from foot to foot. Their hands flap all over the
place unless they clasp them together to stop them escaping. When the
desire to flee is strong they shake, butterflies fly around the stomach,
their knees wobble, their hands tremble, their voice quivers and their
heart beats fast.

How well do the three responses work?

Fight response

If you choose the fighting response you may look confident and upbeat but you are never going to form a good connection with the audience so the possibilities of influence are limited. You are quite likely to invite opposition from your audience too.

Freeze response

If you freeze you can often get safely through your speech, particularly if you are not interrupted, but your delivery will be stiff, wooden and boring. Many people do perform in a semi-frozen state. You have perhaps come across the PowerPoint bore? When the frozen speaker is of exalted rank the uninitiated can sometimes confuse their lifeless demeanour with gravitas. Of course, if you freeze utterly your brain ceases to function and you 'lose it'. 'Petrified' literally means 'turned to stone'!

Flight response

At first glance flight sounds like an unhelpful response. After all, you don't want to be caught running off the stage! But flight contains an important element and that is movement. We have already talked about using energy before you perform in order to be able to hit the ground running. Movement is energy, and energy is a vital resource for successful performing.

Riding with the fear

So let's take those nerves that prepare us for flight and look at how you can use the energy thus produced to work in your favour. The traditional view might be that it would be better not to get nervous at all. That's not necessarily right. Fear – if you know how to handle it – doesn't stop a good performance and can actually enhance it. Those palpitating nerves you feel may be uncomfortable but their energy is gold dust. Out of their raw material you are going to build success.

So recognise this truth:

Nervousness is energy.

And energy is there to be used as you want.

If the word 'fear' comes into your head realise that the word is just short-hand for

F eel

E nergetic

A nd

R eal

Welcome the energy and direct it into communication, connection and purpose.

How do you do that? You steer but you don't put the break on. If you are driving a car on an icy road you know that applying the brake suddenly is going to spell disaster so you stay alert and steer; you keep moving. If you are a skier you will know that once you embark on a steep run success means keeping going, not leaning back and trying to stop. To quote Jimmy Dean, 'I can't change the direction of the wind, but I can adjust my sails.'

If you can't change the direction of the wind stop fighting it now! The more you try to fight fear the more it resists; the more threatened you feel the more powerful the fear seems and the more you suffer. 'What you resist persists' goes the old saying. If you want fear to lose its hold over you it's important to stop fighting it and just allow it to be. This also means allowing the worst to happen, and realising that you will survive. It's amazing how fear loses strength entirely when you let yourself look it in the eye and allow it to be instead of trying to pretend it doesn't exist.

Occasionally people even find it helpful to bring to their conscious attention the very worst that might happen. For example: 'If I mess this up, it's possible I'll be considered so hopeless I'll lose my job. If I lose my job I might find myself without money. If I'm without money I might lose my house. If I lose my house my children might go into care.' They explore the fear in every detail and wear out every part of it. Every possible negative thought, they grab it, yank it up by its roots and bring it out into the open to examine. Having done that they shrug their shoulders and realise that having faced the very worst they notice they don't feel so bad!

N.B. Please note that this is different from obsessing about what you don't want *without* looking it in the face – that only provokes resistance and struggle.

> If you hear a voice within you say, 'you cannot paint', then by all means paint, and that voice will be silenced.
>
> Vincent van Gogh

Riding the rapids – going with the fear

Whatever you are experiencing, welcome it, accept it and change it into energy.

'My heart is beating'

Beat on, heart! Let me hear you, let's make a rhythm of it – tum, ta, ta, tum, tum!

'I'm shaking'

Well really shake then. Shake out the fear. Shake out the hesitation. Shake with all your energy!

'My breath is shaky'

Move the breath then! Think of the red arrows travelling fast all in the same direction. Feel your breath travel out – all in the same forward direction. Now take a fresh breath in.

'I'm trembling'

Gather up all that trembling and tremble deliberately. Turn that energy into determination, power, strength, exhilaration. What amazing energy you have!

Thank you for all that energy! I need that!

You might also notice that something strange happens when you really observe what is happening: 'My heart is beating at this rate. How interesting! Let me count the rate ... Now I begin to notice it's actually slowing down. That's curious ...'

You might think that paying attention to it would speed it up but by paying attention and *accepting* what is happening physically the heart rate slows, the shaking calms and you begin to settle down.

Troubleshooting and a story

I don't understand. First you say don't think about the negative stuff and now I'm being encouraged to focus on it.

Yes, on the surface this exercise looks as if it will make you more nervous, but it's about *how* you focus. It's important to avoid the negative stories that tend to leap into your mind as soon as you say to yourself, 'My heart is beating.' The all-important word is *acceptance*. If you do the exercise with a helper, they can keep reminding you to stay with it, relax and accept what's happening. They can suggest you tap out the heartbeats and tremble deliberately and encourage you to follow the instructions.

If the audience catch me shaking, well I've blown it – haven't I?

I think you'll be surprised at how little they will notice. If you play videos of well-known passionate speakers you will find they sometimes shake too. Just remember throughout that it's all energy and that energy can fire you up for walking, talking and thinking! Shaking is fine; trembling is fine; shortage of breath is fine – they are all part of your energy. Once you *accept* them their effect diminishes and they lose their power to throw you off balance. Then miraculously you come out the other side feeling confident and meaning what you say.

* * *

This reminds me of a conference I attended. Jason was the most nervous presenter I have ever seen. He led a support group for people who had suffered mental breakdown and was at the conference to attract further funding. I think at first the audience feared that he would break down there and then. His hands shook, his voice shook and he jiggled from foot to foot. But he had a message – and that was that the support of others had brought him through a nightmare period and he was determined to help others through too. So he kept going, shaking turned to passion, and the strength of his belief in what he did took hold of him and began to influence people.

He was the last speaker before the midday break. The CEO had opened the morning; a visiting professor and a couple of other distinguished leaders had also spoken. But at lunch whose name was on everyone's lips? Why Jason – and how he had beaten his nerves and convinced them of the importance of what he and his group did. As one delegate said, 'What a remarkable man. That was truly memorable.'

So just accept that it's all energy. Focus on the energy.

Strategy 13 – Breathe in power

Let's find out more about collecting that energy and turning it into peak performance. You can direct the energy by learning to breathe well. Breathing supports your speaking voice, puts you in a resourceful state and fills you with a sense of power.

Holding back any emotion creates blocks in your body and the tension from anxiety inhibits the breath. The best advice you can give yourself when you are feeling tense is to keep breathing. If you are feeling nervous and remember to tell yourself to breathe, you will notice how you have to break through the tension block before you are able to breathe freely. Much has been written about breathing for public speaking, often expressed in complex language. But basically you know how to breathe. This strategy is about appreciating that the breath *gives you power*.

The energising breath

Stand tall and relaxed. In order to take in a good, fresh in-breath breathe out firmly first, feeling your whole body release as you do so (release, not collapse: your skeleton stays upright and open). Then welcome the new air as it enters your body. If you allow the air to fill your lungs naturally after you have breathed out most of your air, you will feel it in your belly and around the sides at the bottom of your ribs. You should not be particularly aware of raising your chest high or of lifting your shoulders, though the intake of air might naturally move these parts of your body as well.

As you breathe in feel the positive energy of the breath enter into every cell of your body. Taking your time, breathe in and out a few times using some of the following thoughts:

- Feel each in-breath build like a wave; then feel each out-breath follow with inevitability like the wave breaking. Continue for a few breaths, then let that idea go. Relax.

- Now feel the in-breath fill every cell in your body with live energy; enjoy the positive energy of the out-breath. Feel the power in every part of you. Continue for a few breaths, then let that idea go too.

- Now feel the slow calmness of the full in-breath; and feel how the calm becomes a quiet strength on the out-breath. Continue for a few breaths. Relax.

By the way, your breath is a brilliant rescue mechanism for moments when you fear that things are falling apart. If you forget where you are or lose your train of thought, then move and take a deliberate breath. If you also take a couple of paces physically as you take in the breath that will help you to get the air moving and shift any mental stuckness. The breath brings oxygen to your brain and the pause afforded by moving gives you a chance to recover your theme. Words come much easier after a good intake of breath. Your breath is your ally; it won't let you down if you remember to use it.

Now we take this idea of the powerful breath a stage further. You naturally breathe in efficiently before energetic movement. If you take a golf swing you take a good breath in as you raise the club. If you surf you breathe in just as you launch yourself onto the wave. If you dig the garden you breathe just as you raise your spade to push it into the soil. A breath taken before physical exertion tends to be full and above all purposeful. So breathe in the same way when you launch into your speech or other challenge.

Your breath represents both physical energy and mental intentional energy. Let us find out how it connects with your sense of purpose and gives life to your communication.

Purposeful 'yes' and purposeful 'no'

Find a space where you can use your arms freely and take a big step forwards and backwards.

First energise yourself by shaking your arms vigorously by your sides. Now pause, and feel the energy running through your body.

Launch into a large step forward (too large a step to change your mind halfway through the move) and swing your hands up breathing in deeply as you do, and bringing your hands firmly down as you land on the front foot. As you land, release all your air exclaiming loudly, 'Haa!'

Now think of something in your life that you passionately say yes to or want to say yes to and repeat the large step above. This time as you land on the front foot and bring your hands down release the air into a loud heartfelt 'Yes!'

Then think of something you strongly, passionately say no to and repeat the exercise, this time exclaiming a loud meaningful 'No!' as you land on the front foot.

Now imagine that you are in a typically challenging situation – maybe a meeting or a conference or some moment when you have something you want to say. Think about what it is you want to communicate. Take a full deep breath with a strong intention to say what needs to be said and then, without a gap in which you hold the breath – nothing can stop the breaking wave of that yes or no – launch straight into the words that you want to say.

The strength of your voice might surprise you. That is what energy can accomplish and that is the kind of life force that inspirational presenters put into their words when they speak. It doesn't matter whether the words are loud or soft, they have to have that strength of purpose.

Case study

Su found that the more she read and thought about breathing the more complicated it seemed, and she got increasingly tense the more she tried to breathe well. In the exercise she raised her arms and stopped at the top before bringing them down to exclaim 'Yes' or 'No', and then felt frustrated that she didn't really believe it.

Her friend Kim who was watching her suddenly raised her own arms in the air and brought them sharply downward in fists exclaiming in frustration, 'For goodness sake, Su!'

Su broke off, shocked. Then she suddenly realised that Kim was demonstrating how to do it.

She did the same. She raised her own arms taking in a big breath as she did so and then cut her hands firmly down as if to make a point. 'I *get* it! It's about having something *important* to say!' Her voice came out firm and strong.

She reported that it was the strong intention that worked for her. 'I had to know why I was being so definite; then I could do it. That's the big breath in – the strong affirmation or strong desire for something. That allows it to happen automatically – but only if you don't hesitate halfway.'

Whenever you are uncertain, come back to the breath. Just say to yourself, 'Keep it moving. Keep breathing.'

Strategy 14 – Find your purpose

In the previous exercise you connected your movement and voice to what you were thinking about. In communication a major element of coming across well is to know *why* you are speaking. After all, if you are not engaged with your subject why on earth should anyone else be?

This is not the same as knowing *what* you want to talk about. A short while ago I coached a brilliant engineer who was about to give a presentation to a group of potential international clients. When I met him he was clear about what he wanted to talk about and had already prepared a PowerPoint presentation with which he was particularly pleased.

'Look,' he said, 'each slide refers to a potential problem and is illustrated with computer simulations and ...'

'Great,' I commented, 'so let's hear what you have to say.'

The young engineer then launched into a highly detailed account of his project including complex models. He delivered the information fast in a deadpan voice. The whole presentation was confusing and tedious.

'So, what are you trying to achieve?' I asked.

'Well, it's a description of my idea for developing the engineering project,' he replied.

'And what matters about that for your clients?'

'Well, they are looking for someone to solve the engineering problem for them.'

'What's special about what you have to offer them?'

'Well, my advice will help them build a project that will save them an enormous amount of money in the medium term and will be fast to build in the short term. Besides,' he added enthusiastically, 'it's a beautiful design.'

'Do you say that in your speech?'

'Well, it's all there in the information.'

'Do you tell them you have a beautiful design, that it will be quick to produce and that it will save them an enormous amount of money?'

'Ah, I guess not.'

As soon as he realised that it was his job not only to give information but to lead his listeners towards what was significant and interesting, he completely changed his delivery.

Time and again I asked him the same questions. What matters about that? What's the point of saying that? What's important about that? Why would you bother to say that? And more and more he focused on the point of what he was trying to say, not just the facts but the purpose and energy behind the facts.

Of course he wanted to tell people about the excellent opportunity his design presented because it was great news that they would be pleased to hear and because they would connect with him as the bearer of good news. The session was no longer an exercise in remembered facts; it was live communication with energy behind it. With this different relationship to his presentation he found that he really wanted to do it.

His comment after the session was revealing: 'It's just so *enjoyable* doing it this way,' he exclaimed.

What's the point?

These are useful questions for you to ask yourself about any communication, presentation, interview or meeting:

- Why am I saying that?
- What matters about that?
- What's important about that?
- Why? What's the point of that?

And when you have answered a question, then ask one of these same questions about your answer: 'What matters about that? (the answer to the first question); and with reference to the answer to *that* question, 'What's important about *that*?' and so on.

This will make your presentation clearer and more focused and achieve something important for your state of mind as well. When you know why you are saying what you are saying it ceases to be just facts to remember and becomes something you have an emotional investment in communicating. Feel the energy that comes from answering these questions honestly and knowing why you are doing what you are doing. And listen to how much more interesting you sound when you have a passionate interest in communicating.

Case study

Get someone to ask you the questions if you can so that you have an extra pair of ears to hear whether you are really getting to the point or are just going round in circles. Remember they need to ask each succeeding question with reference to the answer that has preceded it.

Vivienne asked Julio about his business presentation:

Vivienne: What's it about? What's the point of giving it?

Julio: Very simple: I'm speaking at the national conference about the new system we are introducing. People just need to understand it – that's the point.

Vivienne: What's the point of their understanding it?

Julio: Surely that's obvious? They've got to use the system!

Vivienne: Yes, I know – I'm just doing the exercise! What's important about people understanding the new system?

Julio: Obviously, once they get used to it it's going to give them lots more information.

Vivienne: And what matters about that?

Julio: Oh, for goodness sake! ... Oh, I see. Well, the extra information is going to make their decision making more reliable and they are going to be able to predict the future with much more certainty. It's going to be incredible actually – once they get used to it and begin to use it with confidence.

Vivienne: More reliable decision making? That sounds useful. So what matters about that?

Julio: It's going to transform how we do business – across the whole company internationally! Useful – you bet!

Vivienne: So what's the purpose of your presentation?

Julio: It's going to transform our business across the whole world – well worth achieving! Yes, that's my purpose! And lots of energy about it too!

Strategy 15 – Find your passion

> Success is not the key to happiness. Happiness is the key to success. If you love what you are doing, you will be successful.
>
> Albert Schweitzer

So, passion ...

- What gives you a buzz?
- What do you feel strongly about?
- What do you absolutely love doing?
- Who do you love to be with?
- What animal captivates you?
- When are you utterly absorbed in something?
- Where is a special place you love to be?
- What picture or piece of music means a lot to you?

Choose something you love. Then do the following exercise. It works well with an audience so you may like to enlist the services of a friend or two for a few minutes.

Passion and purpose

You have two minutes to tell your audience about one thing you are passionate about. Tell them what excites you about your subject. How is it that you love this particular subject so much? Tell them about your connection with it and how it makes you feel. Relive the sensations associated with the subject.

When you have finished get a reaction from your audience. Ask them gently how it was for them? Did they get drawn into your subject? Did they find themselves wanting to do the same thing too? Did they connect with you?

Chances are that the answer is yes. Genuine passion is contagious.

What about you as the speaker? Was it easy to talk about something you connected with in this way? Did you find that the words flowed quite easily when you were focused on what you love?

Yes, again?

This exercise is worth repeating. Find various different subjects that you are passionate about and enjoy yourself speaking about them!

Remember you are talking about your passionate *connection* to something. If motorbikes are my passion, I want to tell you what arouses my passion. If I tell you I am passionate about motorbikes and then proceed to tick off on my fingers a list of features including titanium chassis, carbon fibre bodywork, forward- and rear-looking radar and so on, I may be talking about motorbikes but I am not telling you about how motorbikes *light my fire*. Instead, I want to remember how motorbikes make me feel and what makes my heart beat faster when I think about them and then talk about that. Is it the sound of the engine or the sensation of speed or the camaraderie? Is it the exquisite way the machine is built? What *excites* me about it?

Passion is a vital energy source. If you are passionate about what you have to say it becomes imbued with a powerful aliveness which draws the listener in.

This is good to remember even when you have occasion to speak on a subject that you are less than passionate about. Whatever the subject ask yourself: What engages me about this? What am I passionate about? It may be that the subject itself seems dreary – budgets to some people for example – but its results are not. Even if you can find no strong connection with the subject itself you can still get passionate about making a dull subject approachable or about connecting with the people in the room.

A financial director of a local authority who gave monthly updates to his staff used to find that as he ran through the figures he sent people to sleep. But when he asked himself what the figures were all about he was able to come out with statements he genuinely felt strongly about such as, 'The small gain you've all achieved in this period is the equivalent of giving 500 of our children a good breakfast each day for the first time – 500 children with full stomachs coming into school ready to learn – so let's not discount it, it matters.' Finding it more interesting himself, he made much more of an impression on his listeners.

Notes

First of all, this is an exercise about feeling. What does it *feel* like to do that thing, be with that person, be in that place? It's not a description *of* something; it's about what you feel *about* something.

There is nothing to achieve in this exercise. Just find something you love and enjoy recalling what you love about it.

It is about giving yourself permission to enjoy it. Some people might say it's indulgent and be tempted to discount it. On the contrary, passion is the big influencer; people connect with your passion and remember it afterwards.

Be reassured if you are not someone who jumps up and down with emotion. Your feeling may be a quieter one of peace or wonder or something else entirely. It is yours and that is what counts.

Strategy 16 – Let feeling in, or not

Sometimes when people talk about excellent speakers being born and not made they are referring to how alive they seem and how easily they connect with the audience. These skills depend on the ability to reveal emotion in the here and now as in the last exercise.

Some people live connected strongly to their feelings and this can be picked up in their facial expressions, voice, body language and other subtler clues such as skin colour or eye reflectivity. These people live in the present with their feelings fully available to them in real time and expressed in their non-verbal language. If they speak about something exciting they feel excited and their voice sounds excited; there is colour in their face and their body language expresses excitement. If they tell people about an upsetting incident they experience again the horrible feelings of the occasion and convey it in their facial expression, voice and body language.

If you are able to express yourself in this way with access to feeling in the moment you have a great tool for influencing and inspiring others, for they are affected by the sound of your voice and your whole way of being – more in fact than by the actual words you use.

Other people live in the present more like observers and their feelings are kept inside invisible to others and sometimes hidden from themselves as well. They are more detached from their experience. When they tell people about an exciting experience they may be aware of feelings about it and be able to furnish the details that made it exciting but they are not feeling excited *as they speak about it* and neither facial expression, voice nor body language expresses excitement. Their listeners also feel at one remove from the experience.

Your 'default' state of mind is most likely to be either one or the other of these two ways of being, though you may access both at different times. Once you understand the distinction you can learn how to change from one to the other at will to help your communication.

Both ways of being have advantages and disadvantages. If you are in close touch with your feelings you are more likely to be affected by the feelings of the moment which may include fear. At the same time, you will find it easier to interest and inspire your listeners. You have access to a variety of expression when you speak with feeling.

If you are detached from feeling in the here and now you can separate yourself more easily from feelings of fear. It's also a good state of mind for getting a perspective on what you are doing, for planning, evaluating and keeping on track. But you have less access to the expressive variations of voice and body language that come from the passion of the moment and therefore in this state you are likely to influence people less strongly.

It's useful to be able to access both ways of being at different times. If you suffer from performance anxiety one strategy is to learn how to step away from your feelings at moments when they might overwhelm you. If you suffer from monotonous delivery you can learn how to step into your experiences and express them emotionally in the present moment. The best presenters have the ability to express emotion; it's a vital ingredient if you wish to move your audience.

Passionate and dispassionate

Stand up and speak about a topic you are familiar with. You can take the topic you used for the last exercise if you like and as before speak with passion on the subject.

Then pause and take a step backwards. Imagine that you have left your passionate self in front of you on the spot where you were talking just previously and are now in a position where you are able to observe it.

From this observer position speak a little further on your topic, but from an impartial point of view.

If you like, step forward once more and 're-enter' the passionate zone of your feelings to continue your talk from that perspective.

Observe the differences between the two ways of being. Just changing this one element will probably affect your posture, tone of voice, body language and even your choice of words and language structure.

Troubleshooting and a story

I found it difficult to be passionate in the previous exercise, so I haven't a secure starting point.

Then start the exercise speaking in the detached observer position instead. In this position you will find that you don't use the pronoun 'I' very much, but instead speak in a more disinterested way with impersonal observations. From there step forward into the position where you access feeling. Here the language is more personal – for example, 'I feel ...', 'I like ...', 'I care ...' – and more connected with your senses of touch, taste, smell, sight and sound. Make sure the two positions are different from each other. If it helps, when you practise stepping into the 'feeling' place access a strong feeling, like anger, excitement or determination.

The first part is all right because it's just like the last exercise, but I really don't understand this step backwards and leaving passion on the spot.

When you step back that part is similar to the exercise in Strategy 3 where you imagined that you were looking at yourself on a cinema screen. You just become an impartial observer. You can also move your head back a little as if you are focusing on something farther away.

The time I'm most likely to access my emotions is when I'm scared!

Then use that. Start the exercise with remembering a speaking occasion when you were feeling scared. Then step back out of it mentally and leave all the negative emotions behind. Become an observer separated from the feeling.

I tried that actually, but still felt scared.

Then step even further back until you are a good distance away. Imagine you are watching a film on a tiny screen. When you no longer have the scared feeling because the image is so small and far away, then continue to speak – as an impartial observer. Keep your head high.

Yes, I tried that, and what really surprised me was that I could speak much more fluently when I was the observer. I felt more official and found myself using impersonal terms like 'It has been decided ...' and 'It was considered that ...' and more long words. It really began to flow!

That's great. You might think you would be more eloquent when you are in touch with passion – that is the case for some people – but many speakers find that the words flow more easily when they feel less inhibited by personal involvement.

* * *

On the other hand, many professionals mistrust passion, thinking it makes them vulnerable. But, as we have seen, letting down the mask of the role can be more powerful than maintaining a pose of strength. Hillary Clinton was a strong campaigner during the 2008 US presidential campaign but was often referred to as 'the ice maiden' because of her programmed delivery. In New Hampshire she was asked, 'How do you do it?' from a female photographer in the audience, and the question clearly got to her. Her voice broke and her eyes welled with tears as she confessed, 'You know, this is very personal for me. It's not just political, it's not just public ... I see what is happening and we have to reverse it.' That glimpse of real human feeling in the seasoned campaigner, far from spoiling her chances, made her approval ratings soar.

Strategy 17 – Use all or nothing thinking

> It is not because things are difficult that we do not dare, it is
> because we do not dare that they are difficult.
>
> Seneca

You can't half do it – you have to go for it

In our house we sometimes watch skiing on television in the winter. Ski jumping to the uninitiated is an extraordinary sport that gives no second chances. Once the ski jumper has launched himself at the top of the run the steepness of the slope allows no turning back; he is bound to be airborne and must just make the best of it by adjusting his body to the speed and airflow. The choice is: go *with* this experience – or suffer an extremely nasty fall. You cannot half-do it; you cannot do it self-consciously or modestly or slow down halfway; you are on the run and you have to follow it through.

A scary image perhaps! But it can be helpful to think this way as a public speaker. If you are to speak at an important event, you might find that you want to avoid risk by guarding your every word, expression and movement. But if you try to control your delivery to play it safe you come across as monotonous and stiff and die on your feet anyway. Therefore the only real choice for success is to go with it and keep moving.

Keith Johnstone, who teaches improvisation, talks about how students often go about their task in a half-hearted way in the beginning as a low risk strategy that will attract sympathy from their audience should they fail. It never works. The audience merely gets irritated with them and failure is practically guaranteed.

Yogi Berra, the baseball coach, once famously said, 'You cannot hit the ball and think at the same time.' You cannot control what you do and do it at the same time. The tennis champion Billie Jean King advised, 'Be bold. If you're going to make an error, make a doozey, and don't be afraid to hit the ball.' So just do it!

Meditation on leaps of faith

Every example in your life of taking a leap in the dark is a great model for learning to do this when you speak, so scan through your life for examples of going for something where you just had to go for it (or not) and once you went there was no turning back.

Here are some examples to jog your memory:

1. Feeling scared in some physical situation and then going for it – reaching for that far branch when you climbed a tree as a child; pushing yourself off the top of the black run on your skis; running up to a wide stream and jumping to get across; letting go when the swing was at its highest and jumping off; stepping out of the plane for your sky dive.

2. Pressing the 'send' button on your laptop to dispatch an email that scared you. Letting your fingers release an important letter irrevocably into the letterbox. Signing your name to some big decision and letting the paper go.

3. Turning and walking away from some situation that was finished for you. Saying, 'I'm leaving' or 'I resign.' Daring to speak up in some situation.

Focus on the feeling you had as you committed to such actions, that frisson of daring, responsibility and triumph that told you, 'I am in charge here – this is my doing!' That's the feeling to remember; that feeling will carry you jubilantly through.

Case studies

Tom recalls the act of walking along the top of a high wall in his garden as a child. He knew it was dangerous because his brother had suffered concussion through falling off once. But what he recalled of use to him now was his sense of steadiness and confidence; he knew he wouldn't fall. He described it as a steely sensation like saying 'Don't mess with me'; and he finds those words helpful now as he prepares to speak in public.

Jenny remembers being in trouble as a teenager and knowing she couldn't tell her family and friends about it. She went for a solitary walk in the woods and had the thought, 'That's it! You are quite alone in this thing; it's absolutely up to you and no one else.' And that thought suddenly made her feel strong. So now she remembers, 'It's up to me and me alone; I'll deal with it!' and she feels she can do *anything*.

Anya became a whistle-blower while working in a company where employees were being abused. She remembers the determination it took to knock on the boss's door and report what was going on. The intervention did not have a positive outcome for her personally. Yet, that moment outside her boss's door is still for her a powerful resource. 'I had to choose to do the right thing or to ignore it,' she said. 'That decision to do the right thing was a powerful one for me, and having done it once I know I can repeat it. I remember that feeling and it gives me great strength whenever I'm feeling daunted.'

CHAPTER 6

Let's Look At the Audience

Strategy 18 – Make friends with your audience

> My humanity is bound up in yours, for we can only be human together.
>
> Archbishop Desmond Tutu

We have arrived at Chapter 6 and up until now I have only mentioned the audience in passing. Yet the audience is your reason for being there! Your relationship with your listeners is extremely important in helping you to move beyond performance anxiety.

A successful speaker cannot ignore the audience – even though books on public speaking sometimes encourage it. 'Look up beyond your audience,' they say. 'Focus on the back of the room or look at one member of the audience who seems friendly so that you don't have to look at everyone else.'

Well, these are possible strategies, but observe what it is like if you are in an audience and the speaker tries either of these tactics on you. If they focus on the back of the room you feel ignored. If they focus on one person they miss the mood of the group as a whole and you still feel ignored (unless you are the one person of course and then you merely feel embarrassed!).

Another strategy often promoted is to look at the whole audience by sweeping your eyes with a continual movement of your head from one side to the other. If you do this in a mechanical way any individual member of the audience still misses the connection of genuine eye contact and you just get to feel dizzy.

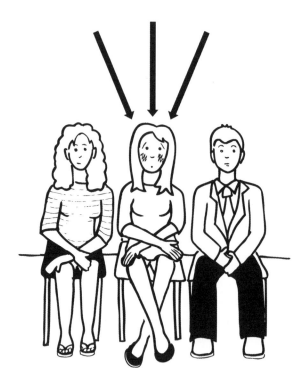

There is no substitute for connecting with your whole audience. So let's look at exactly how you do it – particularly if it scares you.

First of all the audience *is the point*. You are not speaking to yourself for your own benefit so the audience is not there to be ignored. Not ignoring the audience means that you *look at people*. They also look at you. Now if you focus your awareness on their looking at you it is very easy to feel uncomfortable. We are incredibly susceptible to this sensation: have you ever walked down the street and just known that someone was staring at you and then glanced around to find that it was true? Keith Johnstone holds the view that we have a universal phobia of being looked at on a stage.

The antidote to being looked at is to look.

A cat may look at a king. So focus on looking. And if you are going to look at the audience then look in a friendly way or they'll be afraid of you!

If you were introduced to someone at a party you would probably look at them and smile encouragingly. This is no different. Look at an individual just for a moment in a friendly way, and then look at another and another. There's no substitute for direct eye contact.

Use your eyes

Practise making an entry for an imagined speaking event. You have done this in a previous exercise (see Strategy 11). As you enter – let's say stage left – look at the first people you encounter on your left and the people next to them and next to them and so on until you reach the centre of the stage. As you pause there let your eyes continue along the people to the right until you have scanned every person in the room. Look (and feel!) pleased to see them as you take a breath and announce yourself:

'Good evening everyone! My name is Judy Apps, and I'm here to talk to you about the strange mountain creatures of Nepal ...'

Then imagine that you have finished your speech:

'So thank you everyone, I hope you enjoyed that short introduction to a vast subject. Good luck in spotting those creatures in future!'

Look around at everyone and as you leave the stage glance along the rows of people, in a reversal of the process you followed as you entered, as if you are loath to leave that lovely audience, right up to the very last minute when you reach the edge of the stage.

Keep your head up throughout. Get to know the terrain so that you never have to look down as you negotiate the room. Every time you look at the floor you cut the connection with your audience.

If you can, get some feedback from someone. You'll probably find they enjoy your entrance and exit when you do it in this way. Most people watching are amazed at how much difference it makes to your appearance of confidence and their feeling of connection when you hold your head up and look at your audience.

Notes

Do this exercise with someone else so that they can report back to you if you glance at the floor or fail to look at everyone in your imaginary audience. Your observer will tell you how well it works!

Delay speaking until you have arrived at the centre of the stage and looked around at everyone. Take your time and keep breathing!

Watch out! People are especially prone to look at their feet as soon as they have finished speaking at the end. If you do it's like pulling the plug on everything you have achieved up till then as the audience feels you suddenly shut the connection down.

Don't worry if you feel awkward at first; it gets easier and more natural the more you do it.

Strategy 19 – Create a connection

Having greeted your audience you are now ready to think about how you nurture the connection. From connection comes your ability to influence, steer and motivate.

Some experts advise you to be the way you would like your audience to be. For example, if you want an enthusiastic audience you act with enthusiasm. You might have seen this work brilliantly when a stand-up comedian bursts onto the stage brimming with confidence and infectious energy and has the audience in laughter within seconds. But this only works if the audience is *ready to receive* this amount of energy – that is, when it is already warmed up. A comedy audience is there because it *wants to laugh*. If you walk into an audience that is hostile or apathetic and crack a joke at the start it is likely to fall flat – very flat probably!

You can certainly set a direction in terms of mood but you'll probably find it helpful not to be too different from the audience in terms of energy when you first try to establish a connection. This may seem counter-intuitive. If the audience is apathetic you might feel that it's your job to sound excited to break them out of their apathy. In most cases when this happens your mood jars with that of the audience and the audience reacts against you and entrenches itself in its current state. Can you remember a time when you were feeling a bit glum and someone tried to jolly you out of it by talking brightly about counting your blessings? You will probably recall how *depressing* that cheery, chirpy voice felt!

Instead, you will find that tuning in to the prevailing mood will actually get you to where you want to go quicker than by starting in a different state from your audience. It's a bit like taking the baton in a relay race; you want to be running at the same speed as your team-mate to achieve a smooth handover. Once the handover has happened you are free to go any speed you like.

By the way, tuning in is about pacing their level of energy and way of being, not copying their actual mood. Many successful speakers prepare for this by getting a sense of their audience before it's time to speak – for example by arriving early and standing at the back of the room to listen to the general hum or buzz. (Some performers even say that they can smell what sort of audience they have!) Their observations give them

important information about the mood and attitude of the people there. If you do this it will allow you to feel confident that you have judged the audience well before you begin to speak.

Pace your audience first

Practise what you might say in various different speaking scenarios that may be relevant to you. What is the likely state of your audience? Imagine some of the following as a starting point and rehearse what you will say to match their energetic state before moving gradually to the energy level that you want for them.

Let's imagine that the audience is one of the following:

- Apathetic
- Hostile
- Tired
- Distracted
- Only there by compulsion

If the audience is apathetic you may wish to start low key and fairly quiet; if the audience is hostile you may want to adopt a higher energy level and more direct approach.

Don't tell people that they are apathetic or angry: you cannot claim to know for sure that everyone feels that way. Just match the general energy and if you allude to the mood do it in an indirect way using such language as 'may', 'perhaps', 'some of you' or 'possibly'. For instance, 'There may be some of you who don't know why we need to be here today at all ...' or 'I know there has been quite a lot of disillusion about the constant changes and possibly you may almost have felt like giving up. It's been a tough year ...'

Your next step will be to lead the audience to a different mood but practise matching their energy first. Try it with someone so that you can receive feedback on how it worked for them.

Troubleshooting

I acted as if I were tired when I spoke to a tired audience but everything just became very dreary.

Instead of following their mood by acting tired yourself, think about the energetic characteristics of tired – for instance, quiet with little movement and fairly slow perhaps. Then start your introduction calmly and steadily. It's like a respectful acknowledgement of their state rather than a state interrupt.

I'm concerned that if my audience is feeling hostile I will exacerbate their mood if I match their energy.

Of course you want to act as a calming influence. But in fact, if a group is feeling heated about something and is met with a standard, slow, calm 'smiling-face' response they are likely to feel patronised and get even angrier. If your audience is feeling strongly about a situation, a strong introduction will give them confidence that you have recognised their feeling. Again, be careful not to copy the angry mood but to use the powerful energy that characterises hostility. As soon as you've established a connection at their level of energy you can begin to move towards a different pace.

Strategy 20 – Lead the audience

Once you have built a connection with your audience by getting into a similar energetic state then – and only then – you have the potential to exert influence. How does it work? Well, when you are walking happily at the same speed with a friend they tend to keep in step with you without even being aware of it if you gradually go slower or increase your pace. Something similar happens with states of mind.

After you have paced the energy of the audience's mood then move gradually towards the frame of mind you want for them. If you progressively increase your energy to become enthusiastic about what you are talking about the audience will follow your enthusiasm. If you gradually become thoughtful and quiet about something the audience will too. Get passionate and the audience will pick up your passion and become passionate too. You become like the Pied Piper of Hamlin playing his magic music: whatever tune you play people will get in step and follow! The magic lies in your state; if you are genuine in your feeling the audience will catch it – *provided that you connected with their energy first.*

Isn't it funny that we get so hung up about the *content* of what we have to say when our audience is influenced at least as much, if not more, by *how* we say it? Feelings are highly contagious.

> I've learned that people will forget what you said, people will forget what you did, but people will never forget how you made them feel.
>
> Maya Angelou

Leading others

Practise leading other people's mood in low risk situations first. For example, if someone at work starts moaning to you about work or life in general join in the conversation with a similar energy though not actually moaning yourself. If the other person says, 'You'll never guess what they've done now, they've got rid of the coffee machine on the fourth floor, they're always doing that kind of thing ...' maybe you will respond with, 'Oh, has it gone?' in a similar tone of voice. Then gradually lighten your voice as you begin to introduce more positive ideas.

Look out for situations where you can practise changing the other person's mood subtly and give yourself a metaphorical pat on the back every time you succeed!

Then you can try the same process in a public speaking situation. After you have matched the audience's original energy, as in Strategy 19, decide where you would like to lead them, for example to be:

- Curious
- Interested
- Reassured
- Inspired

Begin speaking with a level of energy that matches their original mood. As you continue to speak gradually shift your energy to the state you want for them.

Don't be in a rush to get from one to the other: it's better to speak using their level of energy for a while to be sure of the connection before you shift gradually to where you want to get to.

Sometimes the state you want to move to is so different from the current state of your audience that you may want to move through some transition states first. It's quite a journey from apathy to joyous enthusiasm, so you may like to aim for a halfway state such as curiosity or mild interest first. The idea is to flow in harmony with your audience and not clash energies.

Case studies

Jessie was not happy to find that her conference speech had been scheduled for the after-lunch 'grave-slot', and indeed when she finally stood before her audience they looked pretty drowsy and disengaged. In the past in such a situation she would have addressed them with high energy and exhorted them to stay awake. This time she tried something different:

'Well, it was a good lunch,' she smiled. 'And fortunately what I am going to say for the next few minutes doesn't require any effort from you, so you can settle back and enjoy that quiet after-lunch moment as I speak.'

She continued for a moment or two longer and then said, still in a fairly quiet voice: 'I think this particular area of our topic is one of the most exciting – it's never been tried before, and the results were to say the least unexpected.'

She raised her voice fractionally: 'To get results that were not only twice as successful statistically but cost considerably less – I think even the innovation team couldn't prevent their eyebrows going up just a little!' She ended on a strong high.

'Did they listen?' I asked her afterwards.

'Well, amazingly, they did!' she replied. 'It was as if the very act of giving them permission not to concentrate and stay awake actually made it happen. We just felt in tune with each other. And then, feeling comfortable, they listened and came up with lots of enthusiastic questions afterwards. I have to say I really didn't expect it, but it worked.'

* * *

Ray had always been nervous of hostility and tended to try and placate anyone who raised their voice. It never worked very well and he continued to worry about what he would do if someone interrupted during a speech. After learning in a course how to pace and lead people, he reported the following success story.

He was in the middle of talking at a public meeting about a consultation process they were undertaking before major changes in services. Suddenly he was interrupted. A man stood up and shouted, 'I can't *stand* this wishy washy approach, you spineless people! You should be *doing something*!!!'

Amazing himself, as quick as a flash, Ray replied in the same sharp voice, 'You're right!' Then he continued, gradually decreasing his speed and moving towards a quieter almost statesmanlike tone: 'You're right! It's important to get this sorted. And like you we are determined to do something that solves the problem; and that means solving it in a way that gets rid of it *permanently*. So [slowing down gradually] that's the reason for the consultation. This deserves to be addressed seriously and urgently – to be put right both for now *and* for the future.'

By the time he reached the end he was speaking slowly and firmly. The angry man breathed out with a release of tension, put his lips together and sat down. Ray continued, inwardly rejoicing at the ease with which he had dealt with the situation.

> The greatest discovery of my generation is that human beings can alter their lives by altering their attitude of mind. If you change your mind, you can change your life.
>
> William James

Strategy 21 – Coach yourself

You can greatly increase your confidence in connecting with people by self-coaching.

What – coaching yourself? Certainly – it's very effective. Sometimes you may feel negative about your own abilities but you have many of the answers within yourself. You just need to know how to access them.

Self-coaching

1. Imagine a future event
Think about a challenging speaking event coming up. Then imagine yourself in that future event at a challenging moment. Step into the situation in your mind so that you are in the scene looking out of your own eyes in your imagination. Hear the sounds you hear from other people and the environment and the sound of your own voice as you communicate. Become aware of the sensations in your body as you feel what it is like to be in that future event.

Come back to the here and now

Let go of that experience and think about something different – what's the weather like outside?

2. Now be a member of the audience

Go and sit in a chair as a typical member of your audience for this event or if it is a one-to-one situation imagine that you step into the other person's shoes, standing physically where they would be standing. Being that member of the audience, look at the speaker giving the presentation. That means that you look at the space where you were standing previously as speaker and respond to what has just happened there.

- What is it like from this audience/listener position?
- What do you see as you look at the speaker?
- What do you hear?
- What do you think of the speaker?
- What are you aware of?
- What are you feeling as you receive the communication?

As you answer these questions speak as that member of the audience, e.g. 'As a member of the audience I am thinking, feeling …'

Let go of that experience

Think of something different again – how do you spell your first name backwards?

3. Step into a third position to observe as coach

Move to another place a bit further distant where you have a view of your original position and assume the role of your personal coach. You are stepping into the role of a coach who is absolutely ideal for you, knows you forwards and backwards, has exactly the right energy and style for you to learn well and is entirely on your side supporting you. Get the sensation of being that coach.

- What do you see from here as you observe the performance of the speaker?

- What is your reaction to what you have heard from the speaker?

- What do you feel about the communication?

- What would you like to say to the speaker that would be just the right intervention to improve what they are doing?

Find the resource that's needed

If you decide for instance that the speaker needs to look more confident the next job is to settle on where you will find that confidence. Are you confident out here as the coach? In that case remember what it is like, and get a strong sense both physically and mentally of how it is to be confident. Or do you know someone who is full of confidence? If you know someone confident, step into *being* them and get a sense of how they stand, their body language, their tone of voice, the kind of thing they say and so on. It's like *trying on* confidence. When you have a full sense of that state of confidence then give it to the speaker – either by 'radiating' the skill across to them in your mind or by coming in yourself to stand where the speaker is standing in (1) with the extra information you have gained from the coach position.

4. Back in your original position notice the difference
When you add what is needed, replay the original future event in your mind and notice and feel how this is different from how you were before.

Break off from this

5. Notice the difference from the audience's point of view
Check out the differences. Go and sit in the audience chair again and observe the differences from this position too. Add this to your learning.

Return to the speaker space to complete

You can repeat some of the positions to get further information. For example, having observed the changed experience of the audience you can return to the coach position and see if anything else is needed to improve the performance even further. Then take on this new learning in the speaker's position again and notice the differences in the audience position as well.

This is one exercise you need to do in practice to realise its benefit. For many people it is the exercise that makes all the difference.

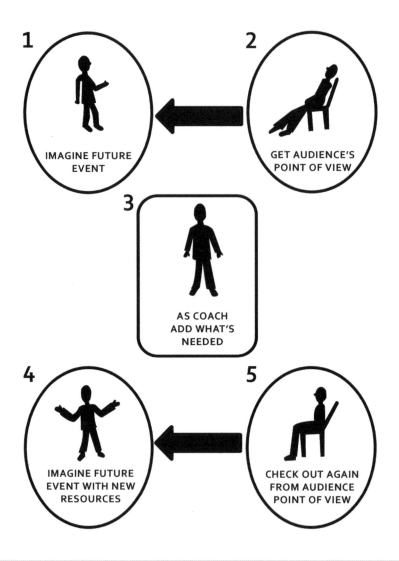

Troubleshooting

I don't quite understand what it means to be a member of the audience or to be the coach?

It means that you take up a different physical position and speak and act as if you are an audience member and then speak and act as your own coach. In each case, you adjust your physiology to be like the person and speak as if you are that person, in their tone of voice, using 'I'.

Where do I find the 'resources' you talk about?

It could be something really straightforward. You suddenly become aware as you observe from the outside that the speaker is standing in a timid way for instance. In that case the knowledge on its own is probably sufficient for you to change it and stand in a different way.

It might be something less tangible – you notice for example that the speaker seems to lack self-belief. It may be that you yourself have strong self-belief in a different context. Then step into that different context in your mind and experience the physiology, body language, voice and inner thoughts in that different context. That knowledge of self-belief becomes the resource that you then give to the speaker for the challenging context.

Alternatively, you may like to think of someone else who has strong self-belief, and then you step into *being* them, adopting their manner, body language, voice and way of thinking and feeling. This physical and mental way of being becomes the resource that you 'give' to the speaker.

There isn't much difference between the experience of being the speaker and being the coach – I still have the same old thoughts that I always have when I think about myself as a speaker.

The positions need to look and sound different – otherwise you haven't taken a different perspective and there's nothing new to add to the system. Try stepping further away to detach yourself completely from the emotions experienced in the first position. In addition, take more time to consider what would be the best coach for you, and adopt the physical way of being of that coach.

The resources you are looking for can be rational, physical or emotional, so ask questions that elicit these different aspects, such as:

- What are you experiencing here?
- What are you thinking?
- What are you seeing and hearing?
- What are you feeling?
- What are you aware of?

Often just one of these questions will unlock an important element to help you. It may be that you are used to taking a logical approach when you think about your performance and discovering the coach's feeling about it will be enlightening; or it may be that the distance and perspective of the coach will allow you to distance yourself from emotion and see the bigger picture. We are all different.

CHAPTER 7

Be Yourself

I was once afraid of people saying, 'Who does she think she
is?' Now I have the courage to stand and say, 'This is who I am.'

Oprah Winfrey

Strategy 22 – Connect with your inner self

Be real ... or as my mother used to say to me in encouragement, 'Just be
yourself'.

I always wondered what to do with a statement like that. I would have
been myself if I'd known how to do it but I had no idea where to start.
Who on earth was I? How would I set about *being myself*?

I think this is a more common difficulty than you might imagine. It is
not unusual for someone in a position of high authority to look in the
bathroom mirror in the morning and wonder if the person they are looking at is indeed the same person who possesses the grand title they walk
into work with – be it Chief Executive, Member of the Board or Director
of Finance. As they stare at themselves they ask internally if today is the
day they will be found out, if today is the day that the world will recognise that their daily behaviour is all a front to hide that 'little old me'
that looks back at them in the early morning mirror. Then they shrug off
the sensation, travel to work, enter the building and feel the authority
of their position straighten their shoulders and stiffen their back as they
face the day.

This is not 'being yourself'. If you act stiffly with the authority of your
status people can relate only to that and you sacrifice some of your power
to influence. People often say of someone they find truly influential that
they admire the way the person seems happy and relaxed in their own
skin.

The seventeenth century Zen master Bankei Yōtaku advised, 'Just entrust yourself to your own nature, empty and illuminating.' You need to look deep inside yourself to understand the truth of this. The following model, developed from the idea of levels or layers in the work of William James, Alexander Lowen and others, shows how you might do it.

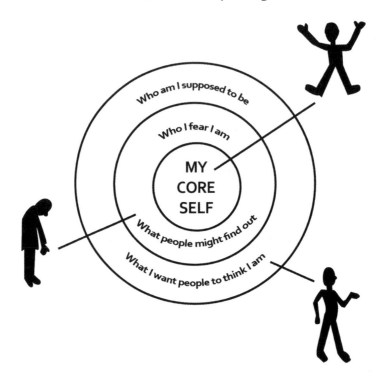

The outer layer of the model represents your 'personality status' – the role you hide behind, the person you think you are 'supposed' to be or who you want to be. It's like a suit of armour you wear to fit in with social conventions and expectations.

Underneath this – constantly threatening to reveal itself – is a more vulnerable part of you that expects to be found wanting at any moment. It's the person that you fear to be but suspect that you in fact are. If you are worried when you speak in public much of your energy is directed towards hiding this layer and fear of its exposure lies at the root of many of your other fears. 'What if people *really knew* – how little I actually know, how inadequate I am, how I don't measure up, how foolish I feel, how many times I've failed in the past, how embarrassed I'm feeling ...?'

Now the outer personality status layer, in hiding your vulnerability, also hides your magnificence. If you dare to let go of the status and risk exposing your vulnerability you have the chance to reveal the much stronger, brighter self at the centre of your being – your 'core self' or soft centre. All you have to do is trust that in revealing something of your vulnerability you will not be crushed. As W. B. Yeats entreats his beloved when he has made himself vulnerable in confessing his love, 'I have spread my dreams under your feet; Tread softly because you tread on my dreams.'

This magnificent core self is who you have always been and who you will always be. It is the self that survives everything and has the possibility to do anything. When you let go of the posturing, control and fear of the outer layers you release all the energy caught up in maintaining appearances and hiding your vulnerability, and you release your authentic energy, the creative space of spontaneity and flow.

That is truly how it happens.

Finding your core

Take a deep breath, and breathe out sighing with a sense of release. Take another breath and breathe out again relaxing even more. Feel every part of you relax more and more as you continue to breathe.

Imagine a light inside you at your centre just below your navel. As you breathe in imagine the light becoming brighter. As you breathe out imagine the light spreading from your centre. Breathing in, see and feel the light becoming stronger and brighter. Breathing out, imagine the light spreading, first to every cell of your body and then beyond your body. Again breathe in and sense the light becoming brighter. Breathe out and imagine the light from your centre spreading to the room, the building, the street, the community, the country, other countries, the world and beyond.

As you connect with the light know that the light has all the creativity, power, compassion and playfulness to be the way you want to be, the very best of you.

Bathe yourself and everyone else in the light.

Know that you are enough.

Notes

Find a time of quiet and solitude to do this exercise. Take your time. Enjoy these moments of stillness.

When you are familiar with the practice you can dip back into it briefly any time you want to. Just feel the light brightening inside you at any time as you breathe slowly in. When for example you are just about to go on stage, enter the interview room or stand to speak at a meeting you can take that slow breath in, feel the light grow within you and say to yourself deep inside, 'I am enough. Me, the real me, just as I am, I am enough. It's good to know I am enough.'

You alone are enough. You have nothing to prove to anybody.

Maya Angelou

Strategy 23 – Wave your magic wand

Just in case you are in the habit of forgetting your magnificence from time to time here is a useful imaginative process from neurolinguistic programming (NLP) for instant reconnection.[1] Think of a time when you might feel vulnerable – maybe it's that very moment when you open your mouth to speak in public and your mind goes blank or some other time when you suddenly feel bad. Whatever the occasion, visualise it now. You are going to create an auto-link that will serve you in your hour of need!

---

[1] Swish process: Richard Bandler (1985). *Using Your Brain for a Change*. Moab, Utah: Real People Press. p. 131

Swiiiish!

First, observe an unwanted self-image

Recall that feeling of fear or anxiety – the moment of your hour of need – and allow the feeling to become a scene that you can watch. Imagine that you are watching a film of yourself, maybe seeing yourself open your mouth to speak and observing that you are about to blank out because you've forgotten what you were going to say. Notice your mouth open and how you look as you hesitate.

Then let the image go for now

Move your body about to change your energy.

Second, create a desired image of yourself

Now create a different image of how you would see yourself if you didn't go blank – an image of yourself engaging fluently with what you have to say, looking at ease and displaying confidence and energy, perhaps with some of the qualities you took on in the last exercise. Be aware of how human and natural this you is – not perfect but confident and creative. Does this you have a sense of humour? What is true about this you that no longer halts and hesitates? Make the image bright and attractive and fasten it in your mind.

Put this image in the corner of the unwanted image

Go back to the first image where you are about to blank out, and your mouth is open and ... at that very moment in the bottom corner of the image notice a tiny dark rectangle which is the second image – of the different you that has confidence and ease.

Perform the Swiiiish! exchange

Now watch as at the very same moment you see the first large image, this tiny dark image suddenly expands and brightens to full colour with a Swiiiish! – completely covering the old unwanted image.

Simultaneously, the old image quickly fades and shrinks away like a burst bubble. One image replaces the other in the blink of an eye, like waving a magic wand – Swiiiish! Open your eyes and look around.

Repeat the Swiiish!

Now run through the sequence again: See the old image → Swiiiish! See the expanded new image → Open your eyes and look around. Repeat the sequence three, four or five times. Try it a few more times faster. Create a habit.

What happens the next time you get the unwanted image? Instantly, the dark image in the corner expands quickly to fill the screen completely with the brilliant desired image. Swiiiish!

Looking ahead

The direction is set and it happens every time. You can no longer see the unwanted image without an instant Swiiiish! as the tiny image in the corner expands instantly to fill the screen with the confident you image. And so it will happen each time you make such unwanted pictures in the future, any time, every time, the tiny new image will expand – Swiiiish!

Troubleshooting

As soon as I recall a terrible experience in public speaking I feel bad – I don't even want to create an image of it.

Think of it as a short ordeal in the service of scientific experiment and successful results! As soon as you have a picture of the image move your body around to get rid of it and let it go. Then move on to the next stage.

The images are not very clear so I'm not sure the exercise will work.

Many of us don't see images very clearly; that doesn't matter at all; it will still work. Act *as if* you are seeing clearly.

There is also an auditory version of this exercise that you can try where you replace internal dialogue you don't want with new positive dialogue. The moment you hear the unwanted dialogue you switch down the volume on it or send it down an imaginary plughole and simultaneously turn up the volume on the positive dialogue which replaces it and surrounds you with its sound.

Why does the exercise ask me to repeat the sequence faster? It just becomes a jumble.

Well, remember that it's important to create a small gap between each repetition however fast you do it – you can blank the screen instead of looking around if you prefer. But the fact that the sequence is too fast is exactly the point – it becomes too fast for your conscious mind to keep up with and as a result your unconscious mind takes over. This is exactly what you want.

Incidentally, NLP offers other resources for overcoming fear including some for tackling extreme or deep-seated fear. You can find details of a couple of these processes, the Phobia Cure and Change Personal History, in the *NLP Workbook* by Joseph O'Connor.[2]

Strategy 24 – Play, seriously!

It's important to take this strategy seriously, so here are some weighty quotes from throughout the ages about it:

> Man is most nearly himself when he achieves the seriousness of a child at play.
>
> Heraclitus

> In every real man a child is hidden that wants to play.
>
> Friedrich Nietzsche

---

[2] Joseph O'Connor (2001). *NLP Workbook: A Practical Guide To Achieving the Results You Want*. London: Thorsons.

Angels can fly because they take themselves lightly.

G. K. Chesterton

The creation of something new is not accomplished by the intellect but by the play instinct.

Carl Jung

Creative people are curious, flexible, persistent, and independent with a tremendous spirit of adventure and a love of play.

Henri Matisse

At one period in my life I had a job driving a minibus. One day I drove a film crew to a recording session for a new series of management videos featuring the *Monty Python* comedian John Cleese. I slipped in quietly to watch the film recording and witnessed four takes of the same two-minute scene. The first take went well and John Cleese employed his humour to good effect. On the second take he repeated all the lines as scripted but put in some new facial expressions and movements. It was very funny and made the film crew laugh. On the third take he put different emphasis on some of the words and paused at different places. Not only did the bystanders laugh but his fellow actors found this so funny they struggled to keep a straight face as they played their parts in the scene. On the fourth take he did something subtly different again and caused a riot as actors and audience burst into laughter interrupting the scene.

I've never forgotten this experience. John Cleese 'played' at working and had his own way of making every take different and interesting. He never repeated, he always *recreated* and made something new. He was playing and learning every single time.

Playing is very different from getting things right. It always has a bit of the spirit of invention about it even when we are repeating an activity. Maybe that's why children's playtime is called recreation. Top musicians understand this well. No two performances of a piece are ever identical.

Somebody told me how they use playful humour whenever they are giving themselves a hard time. As soon as they start self-talking negatively inside they change the negative inner tone into a high nasal voice that makes them laugh. It's a good strategy; inner demons like to fight but just hate being laughed at. Make fun of them and they fade away.

Stephen Nachmanovitch in his book *Free Play: Improvisation in Life and Art* quotes the word 'galumphing' as used by the anthropologist Stephen Miller. What is galumphing? According to Nachmanovitch it is the 'rambunctious and seemingly inexhaustible play-energy apparent in puppies, kittens, children, baby baboons … We galumph when we skip instead of walk, when we take the scenic route instead of the efficient one.'[3]

So what can you do in public speaking that is the equivalent of skipping instead of walking? How might you galumph?

---

[3] Stephen Nachmanovitch (1993). *Free Play: Power of Improvisation in Life and the Arts.* New York: Jeremy P. Tarcher. p. 43

Well, take yourself less seriously for one. And take your audience less seriously for two. And think about entertaining yourself. That's three!

> Laugh at yourself and at life as your default reaction.
> Thomas Leonard, coach and trainer

I once coached a financial expert who gave company reports from time to time.

'They're really boring,' he said.

'Who finds them boring,' I asked

'I do!' he replied.

Don't bore yourself, whatever you do!

Entertain yourself

Take some presentation or speech that you plan to give.

Think of ten silly and not so silly ways to make it different and interesting while still maintaining the original subject. Here are some ideas, but only to get you started:

- Say what you have to say in a very loud voice – as a priest or football coach or politician.

- Say everything you have to say as if to a group of eight year olds.

- Say your speech while dancing up and down.

- Say your speech in a loud whisper as if you were telling someone a secret.

- Think of a metaphor or simile to fit what you have to say. 'Our accounting results are like a whirlwind ...' Expand on the theme.

- Express what you have to say as if you are very angry or surprised or amused.

- After every fact in your speech say, 'Which reminds me of the time that ...' and tell a story.

If possible do this exercise with one or two friends to add to your ideas and provide an audience. Even better, take it in turns to think up scenarios for each other.

After you have played like this for a while think about what has been useful and what features might be adapted to improve your final presentation. For example, you might not want to speak like a football coach, but the greater volume and emphasis you used when acting as one may have improved your delivery and given you increased confidence.

However, don't let this rationalisation after the event lead your play! Saying 'I want you to speak louder with more emphasis and increased confidence' won't achieve such a good result at all. Remember it's playtime!

And realise that these new ways of doing things are all parts of you; you are this *and* this *and* this. Okay, you might consider yourself to be a gentle, unassuming person; that doesn't mean you don't have the ability to laugh, cry, shout or dance! You might feel you have a heavy weight of responsibility on your shoulders; that doesn't mean you can't scream or do a silly walk. You have the potential to be whoever you want to be! What stops you?

> Dance like there's nobody watching
> Love like you'll never be hurt,
> Sing like there's nobody listening,
> And live like it's heaven on earth.
>
> William W. Purkey

Case study

Lee was someone who had always thought it important to maintain tight control over his delivery. When he had this exercise explained to him in a workshop he felt critical and apprehensive in equal measure. But working in a group of three he had the experience of watching someone else do it first, and actually quite enjoyed helping to think up crazy scenarios for the others though he couldn't imagine how it might be useful to him in any way.

When it came to his turn, his colleagues asked him to present his material to them like someone energetically demonstrating and selling kitchen products in a noisy market. Willing by now to play the game, he threw himself into a loud, lively demonstration without any thought that the play might be useful.

The others reacted with laughter and applause, and suddenly Lee realised that in his serious world of work he had *never* had an enthusiastic response to a speech in his life before. This was a first – and he loved it and wanted more of it. He became more aware of the passive, even bored, response he had always had when he'd spoken in public in the past. This was a defining moment and it transformed his attitude to presenting.

Taking that important revelation away with him, he found it much easier to put more energy into his public speaking – even on serious occasions – and greatly enjoyed the new enthusiastic response he received.

Strategy 25 – Trust

As soon as you trust yourself, you will know how to live.
Johann Wolfgang von Goethe

'There is nothing either good or bad, but thinking makes it so,' declares Shakespeare's Hamlet. Henry Ford says something similar: 'If you think you can and you think you can't you're right.' Several of the exercises in this book employ an 'as if' strategy. Whether you think you can or you think you can't you act *as if you can*. You 'try on' a way of being; for example, you act as if you are someone you admire or you remember a time when you were confident and adopt that way of being.

What happens when you do that – and it happens for everyone – is that bit by bit, day by day, as you act *as if* something were true about yourself, little by little it becomes true. Every time you capture that confident feeling inside yourself in any situation it becomes more and more part of who you are.

And your belief grows ...

'Well, you can't change beliefs,' someone pipes up. Yes you can.

> If at first an idea is not absurd there is no hope for it.
>
> Albert Einstein

The first day you sat behind the driving wheel of a car you might have thought, 'I'll never master this, it's just too complicated.' And only a year later having passed your test you arrive at a destination by car and realise that you have driven the whole way thinking about something else – not even having to think consciously about something that a short while before was too difficult to accomplish while thinking hard about it! Those who sit in the car on the first day trusting that it is going to be possible to drive make the best progress.

It's really important to work on your believing. Lewis Carroll, who had a way of putting his most profound statements in the lips of his maddest characters, gives us this exchange in *Through the Looking-Glass*:

> 'I'll give you something to believe,' says the White Queen. 'I'm just one hundred and one, five months and a day.'
>
> 'I can't believe that!' said Alice.

> 'Can't you?' the Queen said in a pitying tone. 'Try again: draw a long breath, and shut your eyes.'
>
> Alice laughed. 'There's no use trying,' she said, 'one can't believe impossible things.'
>
> 'I daresay you haven't had much practice,' said the Queen. 'When I was your age, I always did it for half-an-hour a day. Why, sometimes I've believed as many as six impossible things before breakfast.'

So practise working on your beliefs (Lewis Carroll even gives us one good method here!). Picture yourself speaking in public with confidence and charisma and believe it. Hear yourself speak confidently to an audience of a thousand and believe it! Feel the sensation of having done a great job! Believe it!

I always thought you had to be good at something *before* you did it. That's crazy thinking because how then do you get to be good at it? A friend Paul told me the ducks story. When you see a mother duck waddling along purposefully the ducklings come lined up behind her. Now how does that happen? Does the mother duck wait until her ducklings are obediently lined up before proceeding to cross the road? It would never happen, would it? No, the duck just sets out across the road and only then do the ducklings scurry into place behind her. *If you wait for your ducks to line up, you'll wait forever.*

> Take the first step in faith. You don't have to see the whole staircase just to take the first step.
>
> Martin Luther King

Energy goes where the attention goes. When your energy is focused on how you want something to be you move in that direction.

How do you do that? You do it with trust.

And what is trust? Trust is not something that requires effort. Trust is *letting go* with hope – letting go with hope and joy, even better! The act of

giving up is entirely different; that is like dying inside. Letting go releases the energy that you are currently using to hold you back. It's like being at the top of the giant water chute and thinking, 'This is scary and probably also enormous fun; I'm willing to find out! Let's go!' And then you let go!

> I don't know what's going to happen but I know it's going to be something wonderful.
>
> Claudio Arrau, pianist

Stepping into trust

You can practise entering the feeling of trust at any time. Just take a few minutes to be quiet, to breathe fully and calmly and to settle into yourself. Now reflect on your life and bring to mind an occasion when you had to trust and when you did everything turned out well. Remember again the feeling you had of trusting.

Then breathe in and absorb that feeling of trust. Each breath in is a breathing in of trust; each breath out is a release of fear and tension and a willingness to let go of control. You may like to say some simple words to yourself as you breathe out such as, 'All will be well', 'I know that I am okay' or 'I trust in this'.

Then stay quietly for a few minutes reflecting on these statements.

Get to know the feeling of trust and make friends with it.

Story

The great tenor José Carreras suffered from leukaemia in 1987 and when he eventually recovered he agreed to take part in a welcome-back concert in his home town of Barcelona.

The moment arrived and he stepped onto the stage after his long absence, and as he walked on his life flashed before his eyes. He remembered being diagnosed with cancer at the peak of his success, and how he had stayed awake throughout the following night fighting a terrible fear. Now, as he looked around, he could see and hear an audience of thousands – in fact 150,000 had gathered for the event inside and outside the auditorium. He felt his throat tighten with fear and wondered if he would be able to sing at all.

Then he felt a surge of gratitude for all those who had come and who understood that he had fought for his life and worked to come back. And he trusted: 'Let my voice be heard and reach out to touch everyone,' he thought. 'May it inspire bravery in them all.' He quietened himself and gently began to sing his gratitude. His performance built to a great climax. When he had finished singing the audience erupted with joyous enthusiasm.

It has always struck me, and I see it again and again, how those who fear the most are usually the speakers who have most to offer. Who wouldn't fear performing if they realise it means giving of themselves? What if you gave your most precious gift – yourself – and the world told you it was rubbish, what then? No wonder we are scared! Everyone who gives a portion of himself knows the feeling of fear. *But that is the very reason the gift is so precious.* We are sharing our being human.

Stepping into trust is like taking a step into the field of all possibilities. Deepak Chopra in *The Seven Spiritual Laws of Success* talks about all the excitement that can occur when you remain open to whatever may happen.

If you realised just how close *you* (yes, that's you!) are to performing magnificently you would shout for joy – you are as close as just beginning – just a little – to believe and trust in your own possibilities.

Let the world see it. You are unique, and only you can do this. When you say yes to the possibility of you, and allow what will happen to happen, the best that life has to offer awaits you there – its magic, its humour and its wonder.

Author's Note

I hope that this short book has given you courage and hope as well as some really practical help in your public speaking and communication.

I'd love to hear how you have found it, what has been most useful, and how you are getting on. So do let me know.

If you want to go further down this path, contact me about one-to-one coaching and about the open workshops I run in London and elsewhere.

There are plenty more resources on my website, www.voiceofinfluence. co.uk

> Love is what we are born with. Fear is what we have learned here. The spiritual journey is the unlearning of fear and the acceptance of love back into our hearts.
> Marianne Williamson

Acknowledgements

Thanks to my students who have shown me many different kinds of fear and taught me many different ways to overcome it.

Thanks to my mentors and teachers, especially Robert Dilts, Judith DeLozier, Stephen Gilligan, Suzi Smith, Henry Morgan, my aikido sensai Piers Cooke – and Ian McDermott who gave me my first practical taste of NLP.

Thanks to the many people who inspired this book directly and indirectly through their writings including Tim Gallwey, Eckhart Tolle, Gabrielle Roth, Milton Erickson, Julia Cameron, Alexander Lowen, Moshé Feldenkrais and Stephen Nachmanovitch.

Thanks to the friends with whom I have walked and talked; and to my parents who showed how to pluck up courage in their different ways.

Thanks to those people who challenged me and gave me life practice. I didn't always enjoy it at the time but it was I realise treasure.

Once again a big thank you to all at Crown House Publishing for their help and support.

Finally, a huge thanks to John who is patient and insightful; and to my special supporters Chris and Rosie,

Thank you!

Bibliography

Apps, Judy (2009) *Voice of Influence*. Carmarthen: Crown House Publishing.

Bandler, Richard (1985) *Using Your Brain For a Change*. Boulder, CO: Real People Press.

Bandler, Richard; Grinder, John (1979) *Frogs into Princes*. Boulder, CO: Real People Press.

Campbell, Joseph (1988) *The Power of Myth*. New York: Bantam Doubleday Dell .

Chopra, Deepak (1996) *The Seven Spiritual Laws of Success: A Practical Guide to the Fulfilment of Your Dreams*. New York: Bantam.

Colgrass, Michael (2000) *My Lessons with Kumi: How I learned to perform with confidence in life and work*. Boulder, CO: Real People Press.

Csikszentmihalyi, Mihaly (1990) *Flow, The Psychology of Optimal Experience*. New York: HarperCollins .

Csikszentmihalyi, Mihaly (2003) *Good Business: Leadership. Flow, and the Making of Meaning*. New York: Viking.

Delozier, Judith; Grinder, John; Bandler, Richard (1977) *Patterns of the Hypnotic Techniques of Milton H. Erickson, M.D., Vol. 1–2*. Capitola, CA: Capitola, CA: Meta Publications.

Dilts, Robert (1989) *Neuro-Linguistic Programming, Volume I*. Capitola, CA: Meta Publications.

Dilts, Robert (1990) *Changing Belief Systems With NLP*. Capitola, CA: Meta Publications.

Dilts, Robert (1994) *Strategies of Genius, Volume I*. Capitola, CA: Meta Publications.

Gelb, Michael (2000) *How to Think Like Leonardo Da Vinci: Seven Steps to Genius Every Day*. New York: Dell Publishing Co.

Gordon, David (1978) *Therapeutic Metaphor: Helping Others Through the Looking Glass*. Capitola, CA: Meta Publications.

Holt, John (1995) *How Children Fail*. Cambridge, MA: DeCapo Press.

Johnstone, Keith (2007) *Impro: Improvisation and the Theatre*. London: Methuen Drama.

Kennedy, Nigel (1991) *Always Playing*. London: Weidenfeld & Nicolson .

LeBoeuf, Michael (1994) *Creative Thinking: How to Generate Ideas and Turn Them into Successful Reality*. London: Piatkus Books.

Lowen, Alexander (1994) *Bioenergetics: The Revolutionary Therapy That Uses the Language of the Body to Heal the Problems of the Mind*. New York: Penguin/Arkana.

Maruyama, Koretoshi (1984) *Aikido with Ki*. Tokyo: Japan Publications.

Milton, Hal (1996) *Going Public: Practical Guide to Developing Personal Charisma*. Deerfield Beach, FL: Health Communications.

Nachmanovitch, Stephen (1993) *Free Play: Improvisation in Life and Art*. New York: Jeremy P. Tarcher.

O'Connor, Joseph (2001) *NLP Workbook: A Practical Guide to Achieving the Results You Want*. London: Thorsons.

Roth, Gabrielle (1989) *Maps to Ecstasy*. Nataraj Publishing.

Scott Peck, M. (1993) *Further Along the Road Less Traveled*. New York: Simon & Schuster.

Tohei, Koichi (1978) *Ki in Daily Life*. Tokyo: Japan Publications.

Tolle, Eckhart (1999) *The Power of Now: A Guide to Spiritual Enlightenment*. Novato, CA: New World Library.

Tolle, Eckhart (2003) *Stillness Speaks*. New York: Hodder Mobius.

Tolle, Eckhart (2005) *A New Earth: Awakening to Your Life's Purpose*. New York: Dutton Books.

Praise for *Butterflies and Sweaty Palms*

I remember those butterflies and yes, those sweaty palms as well. My brother seemed to just do it naturally, but I couldn't, and many failures proved to me that I couldn't. Over the years, that has changed, so I know that a change is possible. What is remarkable about Judy's approach is that it would have saved me so much agony and so many failures along the way had I had her tools and advice with me through those many years.

Now I am able to comfortably speak in front of big groups and get results, so I know what had to change in me in order to become a confident speaker. And for every change I had to make the hard way, Judy gives you a practical, and more importantly an easy to understand toolkit that will get you up and confident in front of a group in a much quicker time than you ever thought possible.

The people who get things done, the people that make a difference, the people who others look to for leadership are great communicators. They can share their passion and ideas with any group, large or small. So if you want to be a leader rather than a listener, get good at communicating with groups of people. I can't think of a better place to start than Judy's book.

Paul Matthews, Managing Director, People Alchemy Ltd

This brilliant little book provides super strategies for overcoming everyone's number one fear: public speaking! Let Judy Apps guide you with ease through great examples, stories and exercises to become a confident communicator.

Arielle Essex, author of *Compassionate Coaching*

This is a 'must buy' book for all of us with presentation nerves which, let's face it, is most of us. Judy has an uncanny knack of putting herself in the reader's shoes and I felt she was reading my mind! It's an easy and engaging read packed with true stories about how famous people deal with nerves. Amidst the real-life examples and rich variety of practical, down to earth tips, readers will find that Judy understands their thoughts and has some real gems to dispel concerns, nerves and abject fear. No matter how bad things may seem this invaluable little book will give you all the tools you need to become a confident and engaging speaker.

Carol Newland, NLP Coach and Trainer

Judy Apps' aptly-named new book *Butterflies and Sweaty Palms* hits exactly the right note for anyone who has ever experienced that sick feeling in the stomach when faced with a presentation to give. At the same time, she has a wealth of knowledge that would make the most confident presenter consider how to connect more authentically with their audience and bring even the driest after-lunch conference slot alive.

From the outset she inspires confidence and builds on her own strong track record of working with hundreds of clients to develop their ability to speak in public. No-one need ever feel alone again with this daunting task once armed with the book. It's particularly re-assuring to see the evidence that so many of the best-trained professional performers experience fear and to hear that nerves bear little relation to talent.

So too, I particularly like her suggestions that 'perfection is a curse'. Trying to get it 'right' is a sure way to fail, and being happy with imperfection offers the freedom to structure and deliver an excellent talk. She says: 'For great performers there is no such thing as the perfect performance ... each one is the way it is.' That really takes the pressure off us all.

This theme of trust and acceptance of oneself is a central theme that I embrace. In the book, Judy outlines 25 practical strategies of which my favourite is the final one 'Trust'. When we step into trusting ourselves we share our essential humanness and that's what it's about. I also loved the concept of 'galumphing' or playing about with the presentation to entertain and connect with the audience through simply having fun.

Judy has admirably achieved what she set out to do by inspiring courage, hope and practical help with heaps of easy to read ideas, real-life examples and fun illustrations. I love the elegance, accessibility and clarity of this book and shall certainly be recommending it to clients and colleagues alike.

Kate Burton, coach and author of *Live Life. Love Work* and 'For Dummies' guides to NLP, coaching and confidence.